HOW TO PLAN AND LEAD YOUR OWN COLLECTIVE WORSHIP

A guide book for children and young people

PATRICIA AINGE

kevin
mayhew

For my husband, Peter, who always
supports me in everything I do.

kevin
mayhew

First published in Great Britain in 2016 by Kevin Mayhew Ltd
Buxhall, Stowmarket, Suffolk IP14 3BW
Tel: +44 (0) 1449 737978 Fax: +44 (0) 1449 737834
E-mail: info@kevinmayhew.com

www.kevinmayhew.com

9 8 7 6 5 4 3 2 1 0

ISBN 978 1 84867 838 5
Catalogue No. 1501516

Cover design by Rob Mortonson
© Image used under licence from Shutterstock Inc.
Edited by Virginia Rounding
Typeset by Angela Selfe

Printed and bound in Great Britain

Contents

About the author

Married, with three children and four grandsons of her own, Patricia Ainge worked in Catholic schools for twenty five years, which has given her a great deal of experience with children. Religious education was a key part of her role throughout her teaching career. Now retired, she spends her time with family, doing consultancy work in schools and writing.

Patricia has an extensive background in liturgy, having worked in schools, in her own parish and in the Diocese of Leeds. She was a member of the Diocesan Council for Liturgy and the Council of Laity for many years and has taken on different roles at different times within her own parish. These have included being part of the liturgy group, a creation spirituality group and also catechesis for sacramental preparation. She has a particular interest and expertise in liturgical dance, working with both adults and children to enhance prayer and liturgy.

Introduction

Explaining the book
(The adult bit!)

Planning and leading collective worship is an important step in children's faith development. It allows them to speak and respond to God and to the things that are happening in their own lives and the lives of others in a unique way. It helps children to acquire religious maturity. Wherever the setting, whether school or church, when children feel ownership of their worship, there is an increased likelihood that they will sustain interest in it and see its relevance to their lives as they grow up. Encouraging children to be both creative and active in their own worship will help them to develop an understanding of the language and ritual of worship and liturgy in the Church.

Planning and leading others in collective worship is also immensely rewarding, and enabling our children to do it themselves gives them a sense of achievement and satisfaction that is hard to equal.

Two problems

Our faith schools, children's worship groups, Junior Church groups and so on, do an excellent job in providing children with the religious literacy they need to be able to plan collective worship. All they need is a format and a guide to using that religious literacy to help them get started. They need to know where to begin.

That, however, is often a stumbling block because it is not easy to know where to begin. How do we help children to develop their understanding of worship to a point where they feel confident to plan their own? How do we help them to organise the rich tapestry of elements that make up worship to create an act of collective worship for people to share?

This might not be such a problem if it were not combined with a second which is an issue for all people both in school and in church – and that is time.

Having recently retired from teaching in a primary school, I understand that one of the biggest enemies in the classroom is time (or the lack of it) – time to fit in all the subjects, time to do justice to all the topics and time to make learning fun for children. Where then does a hard-pressed teacher find time to do justice to the wealth of component parts that make up worship? And it is not only in the classroom that time is a problem when planning worship with children. In church, children are often taken out of the main service for specific work aimed at their age group and, again, time is constrained. They often have to be back in the service at a certain point.

What this book will do

This book is intended to overcome these two problems. It is a guide written specifically for children, showing them how to plan and then lead their own acts of collective worship. It does this by helping children to more fully understand the framework of collective worship and showing them how to interweave their religious knowledge and their everyday experiences to create meaningful worship.

How is the book organised?

While this introduction is aimed at the adults who will support them as they embark upon this learning journey, the bulk of the book is aimed at the children themselves. It is written as a step-by-step *how to* guide and, in this way, hopes to provide some solution to the ever-present problem of time by enabling children to work through it, preferably in groups, with minimal adult support.

It starts by equipping children with what I have called the basic building blocks of collective worship. These are divided into two groups – those you need in all collective worship and those you can choose to include. Once children have read and understood these, then the idea of the structure of collective worship is described. Armed with both of these, children are then guided through choosing a theme and then making a plan for their own collective worship.

It then provides a set of resources which they can use to give them confidence as they begin to plan their own collective worship.

Finally the book returns to you, the adults, and offers resources for you to use to support them as they make this journey.

The book is primarily for use in schools and will be most suited to years 5, 6 and 7. This does not mean that there is no place for younger children to be included in planning and leading worship, and there is a section at the end which explores how younger children can be involved.

There will be other places where the book can be used, however. It could be used in church where planning liturgy would encourage children to be active members of their parish and, where parents want to encourage their children to take an active part in family prayer life, it could also be used in the home.

How to use the book

Before our children can begin to take responsibility for planning worship, we have to introduce the idea to them that they **can** do it. So how do we do that? We all have our own gifts and styles when sharing our religious experience with children. What suits one person may not suit another. For this reason, there follow several ways to introduce to children the idea of planning and leading collective worship.

Different scenarios also require different responses, although some ideas will suit all situations so, while this section is divided by setting, nothing is exclusive and ideas can be interchanged. Creative teachers and catechists who spend their lives thinking of the best way to explain things to children will have many ideas of their own, so the following are only suggestions as to how the content of the book could be introduced.

The book is mainly to support Christian worship but, while it makes references to *church*, it is not referring to a particular denomination unless specified and the content is equally suitable for schools that are non-denominational.

The school setting

As previously stated, time is a major issue in school. In a faith school, time for collective worship is added to an already overcrowded timetable which makes it difficult for teachers and adults in the classroom to allow children the time and space to be creative, to plan and do the background work they need to prepare collective worship for others to share. While this book is intended to help solve that problem by providing a tuition guide for children to use themselves, you will need to introduce it to them. This could be done in a number of ways.

- *You could just hand it over to children*

  The majority of the book is aimed at them, including an introduction for children, so you could just explain what the book is about and then hand it to a group of children and ask them to get to work on learning about planning collective worship.

  Alternatively you could form a collective worship group which meets at lunch-times or after school and ask them to use the book themselves. All this would need would be supervision and occasional intervention if they needed help.

- *You could give a whole-class introduction*

  You may feel that it would be more efficient to introduce the idea of planning collective worship to a whole class before asking them to do it in smaller groups. Once you have delivered this, you could then hand the book to a group of children who could work on it in the lesson while you worked with others.

- *It could be used as a whole-class tool*

  You could introduce the concept as above, and then introduce the building blocks of collective worship to everybody. This would equip every child with the tools to create collective worship at the same time. Part of a lesson could then be given over to the children who, working in groups, would use the planning sheets to create an act of collective worship of their choice, using the book as a resource to augment their understanding. They could then take it in turns throughout the school year to lead these for others.

There is a resource to support the above two suggestions in the form of notes for a whole-class introduction in Chapter 12 which starts on page 171. These notes accompany a PowerPoint presentation which is on the disc accompanying the book.

Peer Leadership

However you use it, once you have empowered a group of children within your school, then they can in turn empower others. This peer leadership is an excellent way for children to consolidate their skills and to enable others to do the same.

If you work in partnership with other schools, e.g. as part of an Academy chain, skills can be passed on from children to children between the schools.

The church setting

The approach in church depends on when you are working with the children. If they have come out of a service then time might be more restricted and the opportunity to share their collective worship with others more limited. This should not prevent you from doing it altogether. It might be that a small part of the time you have could be devoted to the children creating one aspect of collective worship, with occasionally the whole time devoted to creating an act of collective worship they can share together. This could be based on the Gospel reading that is being heard in the main service.

If the time is very constrained or already has a purpose, then the approach could be different. An example of this is when children are withdrawn from the main service for Children's Liturgy in the Catholic Mass. The purpose of withdrawing the children is for them to hear and reflect upon the readings and particularly the Gospel of that Mass. Trying to create their own collective worship would clearly not fulfil that purpose but focusing on the aspect *Explaining the Word* would be most appropriate. While you will still need to give input, children will very soon get used to thinking about the meaning of the readings for themselves.

If you have a children's worship group or another group that meets at a different time in the church then it is possible to take more time and focus more directly on creating collective worship.

Another opportunity in church is found when you have a group that is meeting for a specific purpose, such as sacramental preparation. To spend one session creating collective worship to which you invite their family and friends can be very meaningful to them all.

If you are using the book at home then time is no issue and it can be used in any way you see fit.

Begin small

Until they become used to planning collective worship, you can get them to start small – maybe with a five-minute collective worship based around a reading from the Bible. They can then build on this as they become more confident.

And remember – whatever the situation, it is not necessary to always begin with a blank canvas. When the children are new to the idea of planning their own collective worship, you can start with something which you have prepared in part and ask the children to add bits themselves. Gradually they can move to planning more and more themselves until they are responsible for it all. This model can then be used by them if they try to include or train younger children in leading collective worship.

Finally

Do not be discouraged by the number of different elements that are included and which the children are encouraged to think about when planning their own collective worship. At first glance it might seem almost too big a task for them to begin, but there are two things that will make it easier for them. Firstly, they will already have a rich experience of collective worship. Their school life will have given them a broad knowledge of collective worship which has been planned by people who are expert in presenting things to children. If they are also churchgoers they will have the rich tapestry of church liturgy to help them. They will be familiar with the structure and content of worship and this will give them confidence and a good starting point when creating their own.

The second thing is that they are using what they already know. All of the building blocks are things they use in other areas of school and church life – drama, prayer, music, dance and so on. Preparing worship is a cross-curricular activity. This not only makes the worship less daunting for them to prepare but it makes it about themselves and their lives. In fact, it gets the point of worship. Worship is about life – and they are using their gifts and their experience of life to create it.

So – over to the children.

PART ONE

What is collective worship and why should we plan it ourselves?

You will probably have attended a lot of collective worship. Have you ever thought about planning and leading it yourselves? Maybe you could lead others, your classmates or other children in the school in collective worship, or maybe you could take a more active part in your church.

Wherever you do it, planning your own collective worship and then leading it for others is enormously satisfying. Why?

Because:

- It allows you to use your gifts and your skills when praising God.

- It enables you to focus on things that you think are important.

- Above all, it gives you a great sense of reward when you see others enjoying collective worship that you have prepared.

The problem is – where do you start? Well, this book is going to help you do that. It will help you do the following things:

- Understand what collective worship is

- Know what you have to include in collective worship

- Know how to organise collective worship

- Explore different themes for collective worship

- Explore different ways to pray in collective worship

- Think about the resources you could use

- Plan an act of collective worship for you to lead.

Tools to help you

Near the back of the book is a set of sheets which you can use to plan your own collective worship once you feel confident. These are set out in different ways because we are all different and different ones will appeal to different people.

Finally, there are several acts of collective worship that are semi-prepared and just need you to add a few things to make them personal. You may feel confident enough to go straight into planning your own worship from scratch, but if you want a bit of help to give you confidence as you start, then you can use these.

So first . . .

What is collective worship? Is it different from daily prayer and assembly in school?

Collective worship is when we worship God together. It can reflect many different things – celebration, praise, a particular event or season of the Church's year, sorrow or repentance.

When we pray to God on our own then we are not collected together and so this is private prayer. In school, though, we often gather together to pray and this is a type of collective worship because when we do this we are worshipping God together.

Assembly in school is sometimes collective worship but sometimes it is not. Many schools have assemblies on Monday or at different times throughout the week which include a Bible reading, reflection, prayers and sometimes hymns. These are collective worship assemblies.

Other times assemblies are to celebrate work or to give out information and do not include prayer. These are not collective worship.

Sometimes there are special events or times of the year you want to pray about. These can include Harvest Festival, remembering people who have died, or celebrating Advent or Christmas. **As long as people have gathered or collected together and are praising and worshipping God then it is collective worship**.

A lot of the collective worship you take part in will have been planned for you by somebody else – maybe a teacher or a catechist. It will often have been somebody who is very good at working out the best way to give you a good experience of collective worship. But it is fun and very fulfilling to plan and lead your own collective worship. You could choose a class or a group of people and plan an act of collective worship to ask them to share. You would then lead it, just as teachers, catechists and priests or vicars have done for you.

So – where do you start?

The first thing you need to know is what kind of things make up collective worship? What different elements go into it? So, Part Two of the book is going to explain this – the different things you can choose to include in your collective worship. I have called these building blocks. It then explains the structure or framework of collective worship – that means how you organise it, what should come first and so on. This section ends with a step-by-step guide to planning an act of collective worship which is accompanied by an example to show you how the worship builds up.

Part Three is full of ideas and tools you can use, such as planning sheets and, finally, there are a few ideas that have been partly prepared and just need you to add a few things of your own to get you started.

Don't forget though – the collective worship you have experienced has often been planned by people who are experts in knowing what you will appreciate so don't be afraid to use some of their ideas or to ask them for help.

PART TWO

Creating Collective Worship

A step-by-step guide
to creating your own collective worship.

(Signposts will guide you through this section.)

SIGNPOST 1

First you need to know what goes into it

CHAPTER 1

The building blocks of collective worship

Where do you start when you are going to create and lead an act of collective worship for other people? Even thinking about creating it from scratch can seem like an overwhelming task but, just like anything else you create, there are different things that go into collective worship to create it. We can think of these different things as **building blocks.**

The more building blocks you have, the more variety you can include in your collective worship. So this chapter is to explore the different building blocks you can use to create your collective worship. The good news is that **they will all be things you recognise**: things you use at other times in school or in church.

You do not have to use all of the building blocks every time you plan collective worship. Some of them you can choose to include or leave out.

There are some, however, that should be included in all collective worship. These are explored in the first part of this chapter.

SIGNPOST 2

The building blocks you <u>need</u> to include in your collective worship

1. The Word of God

At the heart of your collective worship must be the Word of God. This means a reading from the Gospels or from somewhere else in the Bible. This is because the Bible is one of the ways God reveals himself to us. We know what we need to do to follow Jesus by listening to his Word. The Gospels give us a blueprint for our lives. For this reason they are at the heart of our lives as Christians. Christian churches follow a cycle of daily readings to make sure that Christians hear the teachings of Jesus.

How do I choose it?

You will choose your reading to suit the theme of your collective worship or to suit the occasion you are celebrating – e.g. Harvest Festival. In the Resources section there are suggestions as to which readings would suit different themes.

Where does it go?

When it says the Word of God must be *at the heart of your collective worship*, it does not mean that it must be in the middle but that you should choose it first so that everything else can be connected to it. When you know what your reading is about, then it will help you choose hymns, prayers etc.

2. Explaining the Word

This is another building block that should go into all collective worship and is directly linked to the Word of God. So what does it mean – to explain the Word? Well, it means telling people what the reading you have chosen means for us today. What is it saying to us as people of the 21ˢᵗ century? In your collective worship you will have to ask yourself what it is saying to the people who will share your worship with you. What is it asking us and them to do?

In church the priest or vicar is explaining the Word when he gives the homily. He does it by just talking to the people but you can do it in many different ways.

How do I decide what to say when explaining the Word?

However you choose to do it, you must first ask yourself what the reading is saying to us. What is the message of the reading? If it is a Gospel reading then you need to think about what the actions of Jesus mean for us. What are they showing us and therefore asking us, as his followers today, to do?

For example

Say you chose the reading where Jesus heals the leper. What is that telling us? Well, it is telling us that Jesus was brave – or he would not have touched somebody who had a dangerous disease. It is also telling us that Jesus was compassionate and kind – or he would not have cared about the leper. Finally it tells us that Jesus wanted to make a difference and to help – or he would not have healed the leper. He was not just sorry for him but he put things right.

Once you have worked out what the reading is saying, then you need to make it relevant to today and to the people who are attending your worship. In our example you would ask people or show people how we are brave or kind or make a difference today. You can do this in many different ways.

How could I explain the Word?

Once you have decided the message that the reading is giving us then you have to choose how to share that with the people who are coming to take part in your liturgy. There are different ways to do this.

Talking

You could just talk about it, the way the priest or vicar does, explaining what you think the meaning is. If you decide to do this, then you could share the talk between a few of you. Another way to just talk about it is to write a short reflection that explains the meaning and then to read that out after the reading. If you want to be more creative, you could write a poem.

In your talk you could include a question and answer session where you talk to the children about the reading and maybe ask them to give you their opinions or examples of the message of the Word being lived out today. This is quite common in assemblies so you will be familiar with it. An example of this is as follows: if the reading was about choosing the right kind of lifestyle – e.g. the Beatitudes – you could explain this and then ask the children to give you examples of people or of themselves living a good lifestyle. The advantage of this is that it offers an opportunity for people to take part in the worship in a more active way than just listening or watching.

Be creative

However, talking about it is only one way. You might want to be even more creative and use some of the other building blocks of liturgy to help you to explain the meaning of the reading. These are drama, liturgical dance and artwork and they are explained in the next few pages.

There are more ideas for how to work out what the reading is saying to us in chapter 4 on page 71 and there are some explanations for different readings already done in chapter 9 which starts on page 129.

3. Prayer

Prayer is an important part of collective worship. It is another building block that should always be included. However, there are different forms of prayer and you can be quite creative about how you use it.

Some prayers might be read aloud or said by one of the leaders but there should be some opportunity for the people attending the collective worship to share in the prayer. This can be done if you have a little variety and choose more than one type of prayer.

Traditional prayer

This means the prayers that many people know, such as the *Our Father*. These are prayers that people regularly say and which have been passed on from parent to child. Many have been passed down throughout a lot of the different Churches' histories. The advantage of using these prayers is that everybody knows them and they allow people to join in. They also link you with what is known as the Universal Church – that means all the other people throughout the world who are part of the same Church.

It is important that your collective worship does not become a presentation that people watch, but a celebration that people take part in. Traditional prayer is a good way to do this.

Your own prayers

You can write prayers for people to listen to and reflect on. The advantage of this type of prayer is that it allows you to say exactly what you want and to relate the prayer to the theme and to the people taking part. It is not as easy for people to join in with these, but it is not impossible. You could give people a few moments at the end of the prayer to think about what the prayer has said. You could also have a response to your prayer that people repeat at the end or you could ask everybody to repeat the whole prayer after you. To do this, you would need to break it up and say it slowly and clearly in short phrases.

Ideas for making up your own prayers are on page 83 in chapter 5.

Spontaneous prayer

This is where you ask people to make up their own prayers on the spot. This would be appropriate if you had a small group of people sharing the collective worship with you. A simple way to introduce this is to ask people to think of somebody they would like to pray for and invite them to do so aloud.

Other forms of prayer

Other forms of prayer you could use would be music, where the prayer is sung, or dance where people express their prayer through movement.

4. Reflection

Reflection is an important part of our relationship with God. It gives us the chance to think quietly and to talk to God in our own words. There should always be time for people to think for themselves in collective worship, however short it is. Quiet time is very important but it is also important to suit the amount of time you give to it to the age of the people who are taking part.

How could I use it?

You can use a few minutes after the reading for reflection and invite people to reflect on what they think the reading meant. Another time you can use reflection is after the *Explaining of the Word*. Here you can ask people to reflect on what they could do to follow Jesus.

You might want to give people time to think about themselves and their own lives and actions or their own friendships and friends.

Another opportunity for reflection is when you ask people to think about others who are not as fortunate as they are.

A quiet time where you invite people to speak to God in their own words is another opportunity for reflection.

What about meditation?

Meditation is a type of reflective prayer where you repeat a simple phrase such as *Jesus is Lord* for a short period of time. If the people you are celebrating with are used to this, then you could use this as an opportunity for quiet time in your collective worship.

This type of reflection is not something that should always be included in your worship but should be chosen if you think it suitable.

5. A Focus

This is the final building block that should be included in all collective worship. Your worship should have a focus, something for people to look at and to help create a prayerful atmosphere. In church the altar is usually the focus and in school we often have a prayer table at the front of the collective worship. When you create your own collective worship, you choose what goes on the focus. The purpose of it is to help the children or people who are coming to your worship to reflect and pray. It helps create the mood for your worship. Some of the following things are nearly always found on a prayer focus while some of them are just suggestions.

A drape or cloth

The first thing to choose when creating your focus is a drape or a cloth to cover the table. Churches have particular colours for different seasons of the Church's year – e.g. purple for the season of Lent. You can choose the colour of your drape according to this if you want. However, you may feel that you want a particular colour to celebrate your theme. If you have chosen a theme of nature or of harvest then you might want to have different coloured drapes to represent the colours of the earth. If you are using a table then the drape can be used to cover it. Sometimes, when just a few people attend your collective worship, you may want to arrange the drape on the floor. It is important that people can see the focus as it will help them to concentrate and to pray.

Once you have placed your drape, everything else goes on or around it.

The Bible

You should have the Bible displayed on your focus. This can be opened at the reading you are going to use. You might be going to use a more child-friendly version of the Gospel or other reading you have chosen and so might not want to actually use the version on your display, but it should still be included in the focus.

A Candle

You will probably want a candle that you will light at the beginning of the collective worship to celebrate that God is present among us.

A Crucifix

There are many different types of crucifix you can choose from. Some are traditional wooden crucifixes while some are more colourful and ornate. You should choose the type of crucifix that suits your collective worship.

These four elements are the basic elements you should include but there are many others that you can use to make your focus appropriate to your theme and to make it attractive and prayerful. The following are just some of the things you can use and some ideas about what they could represent but you might think of others that would suit your collective worship.

Plants or flowers: these can be used to represent new life or God's creation. They can also represent growth and beauty.

Water: this can be used as a sign of healing or of cleansing. It can be poured from one place to another or it can be simply placed on the focus.

Stones or pebbles: these can be used to represent the difficulties we find when following Jesus or the mistakes we make. Again, they can simply be placed at the beginning of the collective worship or they can be carried forward and placed during the collective worship.

Seeds: these can be used to represent new life or growth. They can be used to show the seed of God's love that we carry or to represent the potential in all of us. They can be placed at the beginning of the collective worship or they could be planted as part of the collective worship and then taken away by different classes or people at the end.

Pictures or statues: there is a huge variety of these. You can choose between traditional statues or pictures of saints or you can choose more modern ones such as a circle of friends. Whatever you choose, you should know the reason for doing it. Everything on your display should add something to your collective worship and be related to your theme.

Extra candles: sometimes you might need extra candles to represent different things in your collective worship. During prayer time you could light a candle to represent each prayer. Another idea is that you could light a candle to represent the different people who are in your school or community as you pray for them.

Personal items: sometimes you might want to bring something to your focus that is meaningful to you and has a message that is linked to the focus. An example of this is – the theme of your collective worship could be love. You might have something that represents love to you, such as a teddy bear that your parents bought you when you were small. Items like these can be added to the focus and then used or explained during the worship.

Positioning your focus

Mostly we have the focus at the front when we are in school or church but there is no reason that you have to do this. You could have your focus in the middle of the room and have children sit in a circle around it. You should choose the best place for the focus depending on what is going to happen in the collective worship. If, for example, you are finishing with a liturgical dance for people to watch, then the focus in the middle is not ideal as some people will be sitting behind the dancers. Other occasions suit the focus in the middle, however. A good example of this is you could have an act of collective worship focused around carols and the Christmas story at the end of Advent. A central focus which features the Advent wreath would be ideal for this.

SIGNPOST 3

The building blocks you can <u>choose</u> to include but that do not have to be part of all collective worship

6. Sign and symbolic action

Signs are items that you might include on your focus or use in your collective worship that represent something else. They can be things such as candles which you use to represent the fact that Jesus is the light of the world or that Jesus is present among us.

Symbolic action is similar. It is when you do something, often something small, to represent something else, often much bigger. An example of this is pouring water during your collective worship. You might be doing this to represent the fact that we are cleansed of our sins. Lighting candles might represent that Jesus is present among us all. Taking candles away at the end of the service might represent the fact that we are called to carry the light of Christ to others.

7. Music

Music can be a very meaningful part of your collective worship. Many people love to listen to music, to sing or to hear other people sing. It is another way of allowing people to participate in collective worship.

How could I include it?

A common way of including music is to choose hymns that the people attending your collective worship will know. These should be related to your theme. Another way is to just have music that you play at a particular time. Music helps create the atmosphere of your collective worship. You can play something as people come into the hall or church and this helps them to focus on what they are about to participate in. You might want to play music to encourage reflection at a quiet time during your collective worship.

Music to accompany dance

Dance is usually accompanied by music, so if you choose to include liturgical dance in your collective worship then you will need to choose the music. This may not be a hymn but might be a song that you know or like or that seems particularly appropriate to your theme or the message that you are trying to convey. Good examples are Michael Jackson's 'Heal the World' which you might choose for collective worship that includes reflecting on world problems, or 'The Circle of Life' from *The Lion King* for collective worship about creation.

Making music yourself

You might choose to sing something yourselves or to play an instrument to help people reflect or to celebrate giftedness.

8. Drama

Drama can be very powerful in collective worship. It can be used to give a message and has the great advantage of being visual and therefore easy for everybody to understand, whatever their age. It also helps the people taking part in it to really reflect on the meaning of what they are doing.

How can I use it?

It can be used to help explore what the Word of God means – *Explaining the Word* – showing people the message that the reading has for us today. It can also be used to highlight current situations. These can be global ones, such as famine or drought, or they can be local ones, such as arguments in the playground or people being left out in class or in your local neighbourhood.

Different ways to use drama

You could make up a short play and act it out.

You could just have a drama using voices. This would be a bit like a radio play – where you hear what is being said but no action takes place. If you choose to do this, you could have the people who are playing the parts reading from a script and placed at different points in the church or hall.

You could use a still image. This is where you use a *freeze frame* or make a living picture of characters doing some action or portraying a particular emotion. This can be used to accompany the reading you have chosen. If you have decided to just use words in the *Explaining the Word* section, as the priest or vicar does in church, then you could use a still image to emphasise your points.

Another way to use a still image is to set it to music, with the scene changing at relevant points during the music. This last suggestion is explained a little more in the liturgical dance section.

An example of using drama to help explain the Word

When you have worked out what the reading is saying, then you could think about a situation today where that might happen and make up a short play. In the healing of the leper story, which we used as an example in the *Explaining the Word* section on page 30, you could choose any of the three themes and make up a drama – e.g. a drama showing kindness or a drama showing bravery. You could use a few words to explain the link or you could just leave people to think about it for themselves.

9. Liturgical Dance

This sounds very specialised but it is not. Lots of people love to dance and to dance your prayer for God is very fulfilling and gives you a lot of satisfaction. Unlike some forms of dance, liturgical dance is not something that you have to learn how to do. There are no set steps or positions. It is just your response to God's love and creativity. God gave you an amazing body that can do so many things. Dance is using that gift to thank and praise God.

Different ways to include dance

Action Songs

If you are not confident making up a dance or dancing in front of other people then you can start with action songs. These offer a simple way to introduce movement into songs. The good thing about these is that you can stand at the front and lead everybody else, so it gives them an opportunity to take part. You can use an action song that you already know or you can make up simple actions to a song that everybody knows. If you are not sure what actions to do, you could ask your teacher to help you.

Still images

Another way of including movement is to combine still images with music. Remember that the idea of a still image is to create a living picture with your bodies – a freeze frame. For this you need to think about the message you are trying to convey. Listen to the words of the song or hymn you have chosen. Which parts lend themselves to creating a picture? Once you have made up a set of pictures then you just need to decide at which point in the song you are going to change from one still image to the next.

Make up a complete dance

If you want to include a complete dance then don't be afraid to make one up yourself. This means that the dance is your own creation that you can offer to God. You do not need special movements. You can use a mixture of mime and gesture. Gesture is just using your arms and hands to give a message, such as spreading your arms and opening your hands to show that you are giving. Another gesture is to clasp your hands to your heart to show love.

To make up your own dance you can choose any song that fits with your theme. It is often a good idea to repeat movements and to keep them fairly simple. This makes the dance easier to remember which helps to keep it prayerful and stops you worrying about what comes next.

Once you have made up one dance and decided on a few gestures or actions then you can include some of the same movements in other dances. This is called *building up a dance vocabulary* and, just as building up your reading vocabulary helped you to learn to read different books, so building up your dance vocabulary will help you to make up more and more dances.

Remember that dance can express many emotions. It does not just have to be used to express positive emotions like joy and happiness. The choice of music needs to be appropriate but the dance itself can express many things. A slow and meaningful dance can express great sorrow in collective worship about remembrance, for example.

Some ideas for songs that suit different themes are in chapter 10 which begins on page 147.

10. Artwork

Artwork is something else that you can use when building your collective worship. It can be artwork that you or people who come to your collective worship have created, or it can be famous artwork. Whatever you choose, it should be linked to your theme.

How do I use it?

One thing you could do is to choose artwork that will help explain the meaning of the reading. This could be pictures you or others have created showing the message of Jesus being lived out today – e.g. children sharing, which could be used with the story of Jesus feeding the five thousand. These could be displayed while somebody explains what they show in just a few words, perhaps linking this to what we should do today. This would form your *Explaining the Word* section.

Artwork can also be used to include movement in your collective worship. Children can process forward with it and add it to the focus. Artwork can be used in this way to show our commitment to doing something – e.g. pictures of acts of kindness. It can be used to enhance prayer – showing pictures of local or world problems – and can be brought forward while prayers are read.

Do we always create it ourselves?

Artwork does not have to be created by yourselves. While your own artwork is a very meaningful thing to add to your collective worship, there are many famous pieces of art that you can use to help you in creating an atmosphere or making a point. An example of a famous piece you could use is *The Return of the Prodigal Son* by a painter called Rembrandt. This can be used to show forgiveness or repentance. Another famous painting called *Sunflowers* by Van Gogh could be used to show creation or how people's gifts can blossom.

The artwork can be placed on or near your focus and remain there for the whole of the collective worship. You may not refer to it but just use it to help create the atmosphere of your collective worship.

Artwork can also help to include the people who are coming to celebrate your collective worship with you. A few days before your collective worship, you could tell them what the theme is to be and ask them to create pictures showing this theme, or showing what they could do related to this theme. Tell them to bring these to the collective worship. You can then use them in different ways. If there are only a few, then you could invite the children with the pictures to bring them forward at a certain point. If there are a lot, you could ask them to hold them up or lay them down at a certain point. If you want to display them, you could collect them before the collective worship and display them around the hall or church, maybe keeping one or two to add to your focus.

SIGNPOST 4

So – now you have the building blocks, you need to know how to choose a theme for an act of collective worship

CHAPTER 2

Choosing a theme
for your collective worship

Our theme is very important because it helps us choose everything that goes into our worship. While the Word of God should be at the heart of your worship, you will always choose it to relate to your theme. If you are using the theme of Christmas, for example, you would not choose the reading where Jesus rises from the dead. An important word to remember when we are creating our own collective worship is **celebration** because it helps us to understand what collective worship is for. When we worship we are celebrating the presence of God in our lives and that means the happy times, the exciting and joyful times, but it also means the sad and difficult times: the times when we are lonely or grieving.

So, when we come to plan our collective worship the first question we need to ask ourselves is – **what is it that we are celebrating in this particular act of collective worship?** Once we have decided that, then we have the theme for our collective worship.

What could we be celebrating?

We could be celebrating a time of the Church's year such as Christmas, Easter, Lent or Advent. Other things we could choose as a theme might be Harvest Festival, remembrance when people have died, or maybe the beginning of something new such as a term or a particular season like spring.

You do not always have to have a particular season or event, though, as the theme for your collective worship. Sometimes you may just want people to come together to pray. If this is the case then you can take your theme from the Gospel reading you choose or, if you belong to a church, from the readings of the day or the Sunday Gospel. Christian churches have a cycle of readings that you can choose from. You may just choose your favourite reading and base your theme around that – e.g. the finding of the Lost Sheep. If you chose this reading then you could build your liturgy around God's love and care for us and how he calls us to love and care for each other.

Sometimes you might have to use a theme that your teachers or catechists have given you because that is the theme you are following in school or in church.

SIGNPOST 5

So – now you have the building blocks and the theme, you need to know how to structure or organise an act of collective worship

CHAPTER 3

The framework for collective worship

Collective worship is often organised in a particular way. If you go to a service in church then you will see that things happen in a particular order.

When you plan your own collective worship you can decide the order in which you do things, but a framework helps you to organise it and to be sure that you do not miss out anything important. You should feel that you can use your own gifts and imagination, and place things where you feel they will make the most impact and help your worship to flow, but this chapter is going to look at a few guidelines that might help you.

There are certain stages to all collective worship and the building blocks you use will fit into one of these stages. For some stages you might use more than one building block. Using these stages will give a shape to your collective worship and help it to flow smoothly.

The Gathering

The first part of any collective worship is the gathering. This means that people come together. You will need to decide how you want people to gather and by this I do not just mean how you want them to come into the hall or church but what you want to begin with. Do you want a hymn that everyone can sing together? Do you want quiet music as people come together? Do you want a gathering prayer that people can say together? Maybe you would like a mix of these things. You may have another idea of your own. Whatever you choose, finding a way to acknowledge that you have come together to worship God needs to come at the beginning.

The Welcome

When you have gathered together, you will want to welcome the people who are sharing your worship. This is an opportunity to explain the theme you will be celebrating. It might include an opening prayer or a welcoming prayer. Doing this will make the people who are sharing your worship feel involved in what you are doing and that they are part of the worship.

This can be part of the gathering but you might want to plan it separately.

Listening/Sharing God's Word

Somewhere in your worship must come listening to God's Word. In church and more formal services we call this the **Liturgy of the Word.** You can choose where it comes in your worship. Often people have it near the beginning as it roots your worship in the Bible but you can choose where to read it. It is important, though, that you think about why you are choosing to read it at a certain point.

Explaining the Word is most effective if you place it immediately after you have read the Bible reading you have chosen. If you choose to place this somewhere else, then you need to link it back to the reading with a few words of explanation.

Responding

There has to be a point in your worship where people respond to what the reading is asking us or to the overall theme of your worship. For example, if you are planning an act of worship about love for other people then there has to be a chance for people to think about what they might do to care for others. This part of your worship is done in different ways, depending on the building blocks you have chosen. You could, for example, do it through prayer – where people *pray* about what they could do; through reflection – where people *think* about what they could do; or perhaps through music – singing a song or hymn that *talks* about what we can do. You can be very creative about what you do here. While you can place this where you like, it obviously has to come after listening to God's Word.

Sending out

The final part of any collective worship is the sending out. Our worship has given us a message – we have listened to God's Word and we have responded to it in different ways. The sending out is about leaving the worship thinking about what difference it is going to make to us now. What can we do to try to live out the message we have received from our collective worship? Quite often we do this by singing a hymn but you can do other things. You could have people process out, taking something with them as a sign of their promise to make a difference. This could be accompanied by a hymn or music. An example of this is – if the theme of your collective worship has been spring or new life, you could send each class or person away with a newly planted seed. If you are celebrating beginnings – for example, the beginning of a new term – you could ask one child from each class to come forward at the end and take away a candle to place in their classroom as a sign of God's love among us and the light they will bring to the world during the new term.

A checklist

All of the above is just a guide to the different sections of your worship. A good way to be sure that you have included all of the important sections is to ask yourself the following questions.

1. Have I decided how to acknowledge that people have gathered together to worship God?

2. Have I welcomed them?

3. Have we listened to the Word of God and have I explained it to them?

4. Have we responded to God's Word?

5. Have we finished the worship by thinking about what we could do to follow the message of the worship?

SIGNPOST 6

Now you need to put things together to create your own collective worship

CHAPTER 4

Making a plan for your own collective worship

Now you have the building blocks and the structure or framework for an act of collective worship, you need to think about how you are going to put them together. We are going to look at this part step by step. After each step there will be an example to show how our plan for our worship builds up bit by bit.

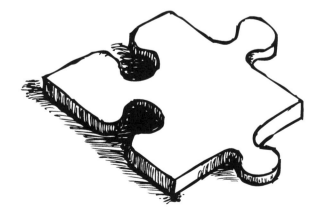

Step One:
Choose your theme

Your theme may be easy to choose because you may be celebrating a particular time of year such as Christmas or Easter. Your school or possibly your church may have a theme that they are following and you might have to use this. A lot of the time, though, you will have to choose your theme yourself. If you have to do this then you could take your theme from the reading you choose or you could take your theme from something that is important to you and your school or church, such as caring or forgiveness. You might want to choose your theme to celebrate a special time of year, such as spring or the beginning of a new term. There is a little more advice on this in chapter 2 which starts on page 51.

Once you have chosen your theme, you are ready for step two.

Planning sheet – Example

Theme: *Kindness to others*

Note: For the example I have chosen the theme of kindness to others. This is a theme that you could choose if you are not celebrating a special occasion.

Step Two:
Think about the people attending your collective worship

This is a very important step to take before you decide what to include in your collective worship because you have to make sure that what you are going to do is suitable for the people attending.

Why do we have to do this?

You need to do this so that what you choose to include in your worship is appropriate for the people who are coming. You need to be sure that they will understand what you are doing and that they can take part. For example - if you are going to celebrate collective worship with very young children, then a lot of silence and reflection might not be the best thing. They will be too young to sit quietly and think about a particular thing for a long time. Action songs and short prayers would be suitable, however, as would short drama sketches.

If you are going to have a lot of traditional prayer then you need to be sure that the people coming will know the prayers.

If there are going to be a lot of people present, you will not be able to ask if people want to pray aloud for something of their own choosing as it might take too long. If there are only a few people, though, this spontaneous prayer would be appropriate and so would asking somebody to take part by planting a seed or lighting a candle.

Knowing who you are preparing the collective worship for will help you with your focus, deciding what to put on it and choosing where it is.

It will also help you decide what version of your Bible story you will use. If the children are very young, the adult Bible is not appropriate so you will need to find a Bible that they use in their class or in their church group.

Planning sheet – Example

Theme: Kindness to others

People attending: Years 3 and 4

Note: For the example, I have chosen that the people coming will be Years 3 and 4. Most of these children will be between eight and nine years old.

Step Three:
Think about what you want the atmosphere to be like

Once you have chosen your theme, you need to think about what kind of atmosphere you want to create. What is most appropriate to your theme?

Collective worship can be

- Quiet and reflective
- Joyful
- A mix of both.

It can have opportunities for

- Quiet reflection and meditation
- Lots of participation in prayers and hymns
- Activity through dance, drama and procession
- Actions that have a meaning – symbolic action
- Using lots of visual stimuli.

Why will this help us?

It will help because, once you have decided what you want the **effect** of your worship to be, you will have a good idea **of what to include to create that effect.** Whatever you choose will help to create your atmosphere. Think about the collective worship you have been to. Which did you find the most meaningful? What did you do that you found helped you to feel part of the worship?

Once you know what kind of atmosphere you want to create, you will have a better idea of which building blocks you are going to use. It will help you to create your focus and choose your readings, as well as choose what else is going to form part of your collective worship.

Planning sheet - Example

Theme: Kindness to others

People attending: Years 3 and 4

What kind of collective worship: A lot of opportunity for children to join in with singing and prayer but some quiet reflection time too.

Note: For the example, I have chosen a mixture of quiet and activity. I want the worship to be joyful and for the children to feel uplifted by it, but I also want them to have a few moments to think about how Jesus was kind and how that calls them to be kind. I want them to be able to think about something they could do for somebody else.

Step Four:
Choosing the Word of God

Now you have your theme and you know what kind of worship you want, you need to decide which Bible reading you are going to use. You will probably be most familiar with the Gospel stories of Jesus and there are lots of these to choose from when deciding what suits your theme best. But you can use other readings from the Bible if you wish.

How do I choose the Word?

Sometimes choosing the Word of God is easy because your collective worship might be celebrating a particular time in the Church's year. If you are creating worship for the Epiphany, for example, then the story of the three wise men coming to visit the baby Jesus would be appropriate.

Other times it is not so easy but, with a bit of thought, you will find a suitable reading. To do this you need to think about what the theme of your worship is. Once you have done that, then think about the Bible stories you know that have that message. For example, if you are creating collective worship to celebrate Harvest Festival, then the choice of a Bible reading is not as easy as if you were celebrating the Epiphany. So, how do you find your reading? You ask yourself what Harvest Festival is about. You may find that there is more than one answer, so you need to then ask yourself what you want to focus on. You may say that it is about celebrating the plants and food that grow on earth or in the sea. Then think about which story from the Bible you might have heard that is about the same subject. You will probably think of the story of creation. So, with a little bit of thought, you have found your reading.

However, in your worship you might want to focus on a different understanding of Harvest Festival. You might say that we are celebrating the way that the food we create is shared so that people who do not grow their own can be fed. Then ask yourself whether you know any stories about Jesus sharing food with others and you might think of the feeding of the five thousand. Again, you have found your reading.

Once your reading is chosen then you can think about what else you want to include.

Planning sheet - Example

Theme: Kindness to others

People attending: Years 3 and 4

What kind of collective worship: A lot of opportunity for children to join in with singing and prayer but some quiet reflection time too.

The Word of God: Jesus curing the blind man (Luke 18:35-43)

Note: For the example, I have chosen the story of Jesus curing the blind beggar. This comes from the Gospel of Luke. You do not have to put the actual Bible reference on your plan but it is a good idea to know where to find it and jot it down – which book you will use and what page.

Step Five:
Deciding how to explain the Word

When you have chosen your reading, you need to decide how you are going to tell people what it means for us today. How are you going to explain the Word? In the *building blocks* section, there were a lot of ideas given as to how you could explain what the reading you have chosen means for us today.

What do we need to think about?

The age of the people you are celebrating with is very important here. You need to relate the reading to their lives. If you are celebrating with very young children, then you do not want to talk for ten minutes using very long words because they will lose attention and they will not understand what you are saying.

How do we decide how to explain the Word?

How you explain the reading depends on what type of reading you have chosen. Drama is often a good way if you have chosen a story about Jesus. If you have chosen a story from the Old Testament such as the creation story, then you might want to use poetry or art to explain. There is no right or wrong way to do this. You choose what you think will suit you and the people at the worship best.

What else do we need to remember?

There are a couple of important things to remember. The first is that you are explaining what the reading means to us today. You are not retelling the story. So, if you were explaining the creation story you would not be telling people what happened each day but would be reminding people that they now need to care for God's creation and explaining that the story shows us that God is very powerful but also very loving.

The other thing to remember is that you must be sure that everybody can hear and see what you are doing. If you choose art – e.g. you might have pictures of people caring for creation today – then they must be big enough for everybody to see. If you are doing a drama, then everybody must be able to see and hear what is being done and said. If people cannot see or hear, they may start to feel as though they are not part of what is going on and they may lose their concentration. In chapter 9, which starts on page 129, there are some examples of how you could explain various readings.

Planning sheet - Example

Theme: Kindness to others

People attending: Years 3 and 4

What kind of collective worship: A lot of opportunity for children to join in with singing and prayer but some quiet reflection time too.

The Word of God: Jesus curing the blind man (Luke 18:35-43)

Explaining the Word: two short dramas showing people helping today – one at home and one helping a charity for people overseas.

Notes: In the example, I have chosen drama to explain the reading. As this is just a planning sheet, I have just put a note about what I want to do and will work the dramas out with others later. I would probably have somebody introduce the dramas straight after the Gospel, explaining that the Gospel showed Jesus doing something very kind. As followers of Jesus, we are called to follow his example. The dramas will show how we can do that.

Step Six:
Deciding what prayer you want to use

Prayer is an important part of your collective worship so the next step is to decide what prayers you might want to include.

Giving people the chance to join in

So far, everything you have planned has been read or done by the leaders. The people who are attending the collective worship have not done anything other than listen or watch. Prayer is a good opportunity to allow this to happen.

As well as prayers they know and can recite, you could have a prayer for them to read. In school, most classrooms and halls now have an interactive white board and a PowerPoint presentation is very useful when you want everybody to join in. In church there may be prayer books or prayer cards or you could make your own if the number of people coming is not too large.

A prayer with a response is another way to allow people to join in.

Prayers that people listen to

They do not have to join in everything, though. There is a place for you to write your own prayers and for the people attending to just listen and reflect. If you do this, you may want to give them a moment's silence at the end of the prayer for them to think about what you have said.

The important thing to remember, as with everything else in your collective worship, is to make it appropriate to the age of the people attending.

Planning sheet - Example

Theme: Kindness to others

People attending: Years 3 and 4

What kind of collective worship: A lot of opportunity for children to join in with singing and prayer but some quiet reflection time too.

The Word of God: Jesus curing the blind man (Luke 18:35-43)

Explaining the Word: two short dramas showing people helping today – one at home and one helping a charity for people overseas.

Prayer: The 'Our Father' as everybody knows this and it talks about how we should live. Four intercessions written by children encouraging us all to be kind to others.

Note: I have not said who will write the prayers or what they will write, as this is only the planning sheet. That will be done later. Intercessions are sometimes called bidding prayers. They usually end with a response such as 'Lord, hear us' or 'Lord, in your mercy' and people respond 'Lord, graciously hear us' or 'Hear our prayer'. You can make up this response yourself as long as you explain what people have to say.

Step Seven:
Deciding what else you want in your collective worship

Now you have the basis for your collective worship. These are the main building blocks so the next step is to decide the other elements you might want to include.

This is entirely up to you and can include any of the building blocks explained in the last chapter. While the choice is up to you, there are a few things that might help you.

The first thing has been mentioned many times before and it is to **think about the people who are attending**. While preparing collective worship is a very satisfying thing, you must always remember you are also trying to give people a good experience of worship, so ask yourself – what will speak to them? Will they enjoy being able to do a lot of singing and maybe some dance or will they prefer quieter worship? You do not have to plan your collective worship to suit a particular person but always give a thought to the people who are attending. In the case of my example, I would think about what Years 3 and 4 would enjoy as well as what I think the theme of kindness allowed me to do.

The second thing to consider when deciding what else to put into your collective worship is what it is that you particularly like or are particularly good at. If you are good at dance, then put in a dance. If you are good at acting, then put in some drama. If you love art, then put some into the collective worship. This will make the worship meaningful and special to you by using your special gifts and talents.

The third thing to remember is that you do not have to put everything into your collective worship. In fact, it would be too much to include everything all the time. Choose what will get your message over and allow people to participate.

And finally . . .

Remember that some of these building blocks are connected. Dance and music are a form of prayer. Symbolic actions such as taking something from the altar or prayer focus – e.g. a plant to represent growth and new life – represent a form of movement so you can include a lot of variety without a lot of extra planning.

Planning sheet - Example

Theme: Kindness to others

People attending: Years 3 and 4

What kind of collective worship: A lot of opportunity for children to join in with singing and prayer but some quiet reflection time too.

The Word of God: Jesus curing the blind man (Luke 18:35-43)

Explaining the Word: two short dramas showing people helping today – one at home and one helping a charity for people overseas.

Prayer: The 'Our Father' as everybody knows this and it talks about how we should live. Four intercessions written by children encouraging us all to be kind to others.

Other things to include:

- Hymns – 'The servant King' verses 1 and 4; 'Here I Am'

- Symbolic action – we will use four candles and light one as each bidding prayer is read

- Dance – 'You've got a friend in me' from Toy Story

Notes: To finish planning my example, I have decided to include two hymns that Years 3 and 4 will know. I have also decided to include a symbolic action which will take place during the reading of the bidding prayers and I have decided to end with a dance. I have not yet chosen who will do all of these things or made up the dance.

Step Eight:
Designing your focus

Now that the plan for the whole of your collective worship is complete, you can start to think about your focus. In the *Building Blocks* section it was explained that there are some things that you should always have on your focus but you can now choose other things if you wish that are meaningful in your particular act of worship.

Including things that you need

You can include anything that you need during your worship. For instance, in my example I would need four candles as well as the main candle I would light at the beginning.

Including things to emphasise your theme

You can also include things that are relevant to the theme of your collective worship. If your theme is *Gifts* then you might want something on there to reflect the gifts you and the people at your worship have – for example, a recorder to show musical talent. If it is about creation, you could add flowers or plants but you could also add pictures and things you have made to show creativity. You could add a mirror to reflect God's beauty to the world.

There are lots of ideas and, with a bit of imagination, you can make a beautiful and relevant focus. Remember not to put too much on it though. If it is cluttered then nothing will stand out and it will lose its impact.

Does everything I need have to be on the focus?

You do not have to put everything on the focus. It depends how you want to use it. You might want somebody to process from the back with something. If you do, then these things could be placed on a table at the back or given to particular children.

Planning sheet - Example

Theme: Kindness to others

People attending: Years 3 and 4

What kind of collective worship: A lot of opportunity for children to join in with singing and prayer but some quiet reflection time too.

The Word of God: Jesus curing the blind man (Luke 18:35-43)

Explaining the Word: two short dramas showing people helping today – one at home and one helping a charity for people overseas.

Prayer: The 'Our Father' as everybody knows this and it talks about how we should live. Four intercessions written by children encouraging us all to be kind to others.

Other things to include:

- Hymns – 'The servant King' verses 1 and 4; 'Here I Am'

- Symbolic action – we will use four candles and light one as each bidding prayer is read

- Dance – 'You've got a friend in me' from Toy Story

Focus: Drape that is yellow to show happiness; a main candle; a Bible; a crucifix; a statue of a circle of friends; four candles to light during the intercessions ; a statue showing two people holding hands

Note: In the example, I have listed the items that I will use on my focus and given details – e.g. for the four candles. When you are used to planning collective worship you do not need to give details; just write the list so that you do not forget anything. Also, I have chosen a statue of two people holding hands as I know that I have one and it will be meaningful. You should choose things that you know you have or can get hold of.

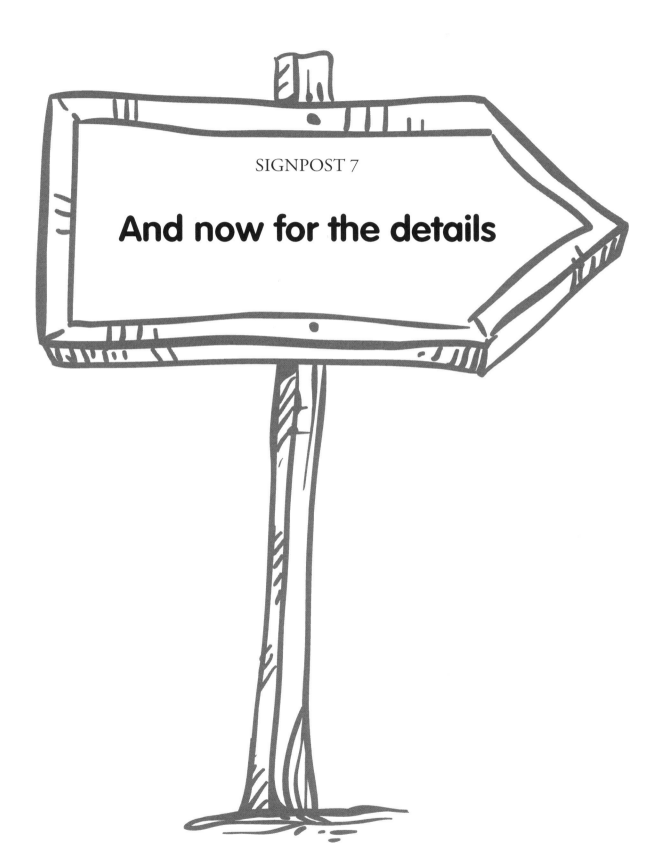

SIGNPOST 7

And now for the details

CHAPTER 5

Adding the details

Now that you have the plan of what you are going to do and what you are going to include, you need to fill in the details. This can include any of the following:

- Writing prayers

- Making up drama scenes

- Making up a dance

- Creating artwork

- Organising your music

- Making a PowerPoint presentation so that people can see hymn words and any responses they need to say

- Deciding what part each person is going to play in the worship

- Collecting resources you might need.

Let's look at these in more detail, step by step. Some of them only need a few words as they have been explained in detail in the *Building Blocks* section. Some of the steps you may not need to use. It depends what you have decided to include in your collective worship. We will continue the steps from the last section.

Step Nine: Writing prayers

Most people will know traditional prayers and you usually do not have to provide the words for these. If you have chosen to include prayers that you make up yourself, though, you will need to decide who is going to write them and what they are going to be about. They should reflect your theme.

How do I know what type of prayer to write?

Before writing prayers, you need to think about what the prayer is doing. Is it asking for something? Is it praising God? Is it saying sorry for something? When you know this then you have a good idea of what to write.

Asking for something

This type of prayer is often called a petition. In church we sometimes call them *bidding prayers* or *intercessions*. They can have a set format and response – for example, they could begin *God our Father* or *Lord Jesus*. The response could be *hear our prayer.* If you want to write these, then they must be relevant to your theme. Here is an example of this type of prayer that you might find in collective worship that is celebrating Harvest Festival.

> *God our Father, the earth gives us many good things and produces enough for us all to eat. We pray that people around the world will share fairly so that everybody has enough food. Lord in your mercy –* **response – hear our prayer**.

Praising God

You might want your prayer to praise or thank God for something. An example of this is to thank God for somebody's life if you are celebrating a service of remembrance. A litany is one way to do this because it involves everybody. For this kind of prayer you have a simple response that is repeated at the end of each statement that is made by the leader. Here is an example of this type of prayer that you might find in collective worship that is celebrating Harvest Festival. The response that everybody would say is in bold.

For the earth which you created and is full of beauty – **Lord, we praise you**

For the sea which you created and is full of life – **Lord, we praise you**

For the air that we breathe which gives us life – **Lord, we praise you**

For the gift of Jesus your Son – **Lord, we praise you**

For the gift of ourselves – **Lord, we praise you**

Saying sorry

You might want to include a prayer where you say sorry for something. This can also have a response which everybody can say together. In Matthew's Gospel, Jesus says that if we are going to make an offering in church and we remember that we have fallen out with our brother, then we should go and make up before we offer our gift. For this reason we often have sorry or penitential prayer at the beginning of services. In your worship, though, you can place them where you want. Here is an example of this type of prayer that you might find in collective worship that is celebrating Harvest Festival and includes a fair sharing of the earth's resources. The response that everybody would say is in bold.

For the times we have not taken care of our environment: **Lord, have mercy**

For the times we have not taken care of each other: **Lord, have mercy**

For the times that we have not shared fairly and somebody has had to do without: **Lord, have mercy**

For the times we have not seen your face in our neighbour: **Lord, have mercy**

Writing prayers can be fun and it is very satisfying to have everybody listening to and sharing prayers that are your creation.

Step Ten: Making up drama scenes

The different types of drama scenes have been described in the *Building Blocks* section. Here is a reminder.

- Tell a story by acting it out

- Create a still image or freeze frame

- Mime while something is read.

You might be able to think of a different way to use drama. If you do, don't be afraid to use it.

What do I do first?

The first thing you need to decide is which one of the types of drama you want to use. You might be able to answer that straightaway as you might have a very clear idea about what you want to do. You might not be sure though. You just might want drama because you think it would be effective. Whether you are sure or not, the next step is very important.

The most important question

Whether you have already chosen the type of drama you want to use or not, the most important thing you need to decide is **what you want the drama to do**.

There are two main effects that drama can have in collective worship. It can

- **Enhance the worship** (this means to make it richer or better)

- **Explain something in the worship**.

Drama to enhance the worship

Enhancing the worship means to make it a richer experience for people. It does it by adding something visual. An example of this is using drama to support the Word of God and you can do this in two ways. You can either –

- **Work out a mime that acts out the Bible reading you have chosen**. If you do this, then one person can read the reading while others do the mime, or –

- **Dramatise the reading with a script as well as actions**. If you do this, you will not need anybody to read the reading as the drama will tell the story. You may want to add a narrator, though, to read the bits of the story that are difficult to put into speech.

It does not have to be the Word of God that you use when adding drama in this way. You could use either of the above to explain or enrich another reading or poem.

Drama to explain something in the worship

The other way you can use drama is to explain something in the worship.

- **Explaining the Word:** This is an obvious way to use drama. If you decide to do this, then remember that your drama must **explain** what the reading means for us today and not just retell the story. It needs to show people what we should be doing in our lives today because of what the Bible says. The example on page 72 does this. It takes one meaning from the reading – the fact that Jesus was kind – and then suggests short drama scenes to show people being kind today.

- **Drama related to the theme:** You may want to use drama that is not directly related to the Word of God and, instead, relate it to the theme of your worship. This means you can put the drama anywhere you like. If, for example, your theme was forgiveness, you might want a short drama to show somebody forgiving a friend or member of their family. This drama could be placed anywhere in the worship. You could have it at the beginning and let it state your theme for you, or you could have it later once it is clear what the theme is.

- **Drama related to an organisation:** There are many organisations that do good work throughout the world. Examples of these are Christian Aid, the Samaritans and CAFOD. You could use drama scenes to show the effect of their work. This would involve a bit of research but could be very effective.

Step Eleven:
Making up a dance

Different ways to use dance have been explained in the *Building Blocks* section. Here is a reminder.

- Action songs

- Still image

- Making up a complete dance.

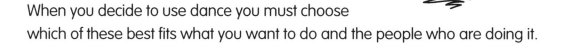

When you decide to use dance you must choose
which of these best fits what you want to do and the people who are doing it.

How do I decide which to choose?

The most important thing when deciding this is to ask yourself what effect you want the dance to have. Dance can do many things. It can –

- **Be thoughtful and meditative and help people to reflect:** If you want it to do this, then you can choose either a quiet song or piece of music and create still images or living pictures that change as the song progresses. Another thing you could do would be to create a whole dance for a group to do to a piece of music.

- **Be joyful and help people to celebrate:** If you want it to do this, then maybe a dance they can join in would be good, such as an action song.

- **Give a message:** A good way to do this would be to choose a song carefully, one that gives the message you want and then make up a dance or a series of living pictures or still images to it.

How do I make up a dance?

You do not need special training to make up a liturgical dance as it is a prayer. You will have some experience of dance to help you when you come to create one, though. You will have done dance in school, so use ideas from those lessons. Also use ideas from other times you have danced – maybe at school parties or discos. If you have not made a dance up before, then use mime or gesture to help you. Some tips are given in the *Building Blocks* section on Liturgical Dance which starts on page 45.

A few things to remember are

- Always suit your dance to the people who are doing it. If they are not used to dancing in front of other people, then make it simple so that they feel confident.

- Choose your music carefully. Make sure it is appropriate for use in worship and does not have any words that are unsuitable. There are a lot of popular songs that would be good in worship but there are some that are not suitable. Also make sure that it is not too long or it will lose its impact.

Ideas for music that suit different themes are given in chapter ten which starts on page 147.

Step Twelve:
Creating Artwork

Artwork can be used in many different ways. Examples of how to use it are –

- To enrich or explain the Word of God

- To convey a message, such as serving others

- To show people doing God's work

- To celebrate creation

- To celebrate giftedness.

You might be able to think of a different way to use it.

How do I decide which to choose?

Like other building blocks, you need to decide what job you want the artwork to do. You can choose from the list above or you might have another idea. Once you have decided what you want the artwork to do, then you can move on to the next step.

Who will create the artwork?

Using posters or artists' work

If you have decided to use art that is already created, such as the work from a famous artist or a poster from an organisation such as Christian Aid, then you only need to decide where you will get it from. If you are using a painting by a famous artist – e.g. Leonardo da Vinci's *Last Supper* – then you might get a copy of it from a book or from a teacher or catechist. If you do this, then remember that it needs to be big enough for people to see. Often you can get an image from the internet which you can display as part of a PowerPoint presentation.

Organisations will send you posters advertising their work or you may already have them in school or in church.

Creating artwork yourselves

You might want to create your own artwork – posters or pictures that have a special meaning in the worship, maybe illustrating the reading or representing the theme. This is a good idea in two ways. Firstly, it allows you to show exactly what you want and, secondly, it is using your own gifts to praise God. If you decide to do this, then you must allow yourself enough time to complete the work. You might have to do it in your own time or maybe work as a team to produce it.

Asking others to create artwork

This means asking people who are not part of your small planning group to prepare something for you. If you decide to do this then it is often a good idea to ask the children who will be attending the worship to produce something. This helps them to feel included and to contribute to the worship. If you decide to do this, you must allow time for them to be told the theme and complete the work. In school this means talking to the teacher first, as the class you are asking will have a full timetable and the teacher will want to be able to fit the artwork in and give the children sufficient time to finish it and to do a good job.

Where should the artwork go?

Again, to answer this question you need to ask yourself: what is the purpose of the artwork? If it is simply to celebrate the giftedness of the people present or to support the theme, it can just be placed on the focus and left there throughout the worship.

If the artwork is to explain or support a reading or prayer, then you might want children to stand at the front and hold the artwork for a short period of time. They might then return to their place with it or place it on the focus.

You might want to add movement to your liturgy by having children process to the front with pictures or posters and then add them to the focus. This might be done during a hymn or reading.

The artwork may be used for reflection or meditation and, if so, then it can be shown on a PowerPoint presentation or placed at the front at the relevant time.

A key thing to remember whether you are creating the art yourselves or using posters or famous artwork is that it must be big enough to be seen if you are displaying it at the front. The only exception to this is if you are having a procession of children bring their own artwork to the front to celebrate giftedness. The purpose of this would not be to explain something but to celebrate the creativity present. The pictures could be placed on the focus for people to look at afterwards. If you have a number of large pictures it would be difficult to display them in this way.

Step Thirteen:
Organising your music

Music can be a very important part of your worship as it can do a lot of things. It can –

- Create an atmosphere
- Allow people to join in
- Pray in a different way
- Support dance
- Celebrate giftedness.

You might think of a different way to use it.

How do I choose the right music?

Your music needs to fit in with your theme.

If you are choosing hymns then you need to be sure that people know them so that they can join in. This will be easy in school as you know what you usually sing. If you are preparing worship for other people, such as a group in church, then it is a good idea to ask a catechist or an adult what songs people know. If you want a hymn to use for an action song, it is a good idea to choose one that is repetitive so that people can pick up the actions you make up.

If you are choosing music for a dance, for a procession or simply to enhance your worship, then you can choose anything that is suitable. This does not have to be hymns but can be popular songs or songs from films. There are a lot of songs that have clear and beautiful messages and would be suitable for using in worship. You need to decide what emotion you want the song to inspire in other people. Ideas for songs that you can use are in chapter 10 which begins on page 147.

Do I need to do anything else?

The only other thing to do, once you have chosen your music, is to make sure that you have access to it. If you are singing hymns, then who is going to play the backing music? Do you have a pianist in school or church? – if you do, you need to talk to him or her before the worship to be sure that they have the music. If not, then maybe you have backing tracks in school and this would involve having them ready and having a CD player and choosing somebody to operate it.

For other music you need to be sure that you have the relevant tracks, perhaps on CD or an iPod and the means to play them.

Step Fourteen:
Making a PowerPoint presentation

A PowerPoint presentation is not essential but it can be extremely useful especially in school worship, enabling people to follow the worship and join in with it as it can provide hymn words and words for prayers.

This will be an easy step for you as you will have made PowerPoint presentations for many subjects at school and you will have seen ones that your teachers have created for collective worship in school. You will know all about choosing your background and inserting any clip art to enhance the look of your presentation.

The important thing to remember when creating a PowerPoint presentation to support worship is that you must include everything on it that you want people to say or sing, unless it is a very well known prayer, such as the 'Our Father'.

You do not have to put everything on your PowerPoint presentation. Things that you say or read yourself do not have to be included in full. You might want a slide to make a reference to them but not include the full text – e.g.

A reading from the Gospel of St John

It is important that you allow yourself enough time to create your PowerPoint presentation. In school this will involve talking to your teacher and asking for an opportunity to do this. The advantage of this is that you may have hymn words and prayers already on your school system, so you will only need to cut and paste them rather than typing everything out.

Alternatively, if you have a computer at home then you could create it in your own time.

In school there will be a system already set up in the hall for you to show your PowerPoint presentation and you will probably be familiar with it already. If not, somebody will show you how to use it.

If there is no system, perhaps in church, then you will not need a PowerPoint presentation and may have to use hymn books and prayer books to allow people to join in.

Step Fifteen: Deciding what parts people are playing

To help your worship run smoothly, you need to decide beforehand what part each person in your team is playing. It is a good idea to share out responsibilities so that nobody has too much to remember.

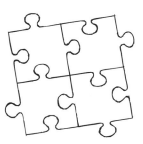

There will be many different things to do in your worship and it is important to decide who is going to do each different thing. You may have decided this as you have planned it but, if not, then you must do it now. Each act of worship is different so only you know what exactly has to be done in your own collective worship, but here is a suggested checklist of things that you might need to ask people to do:

- Setting up the focus

- Being responsible for the PowerPoint presentation

- Welcoming

- Playing the music if you are using recorded music or backing tracks

- Reading the Word of God

- Reading the prayers

- Taking part in the drama or dance if you are using this

- Reading any extra parts, such as leading or introducing *Explaining the Word*

- Processing with things such as artwork, candles, flowers, gifts, etc.

- Doing any symbolic action such as lighting candles.

These are the main things that people do in worship but you might have something else you want to do, such as leading a question and answer session, and you will have to decide who is responsible for this if you decide to include it.

Try to be fair to people and share the roles out evenly, so that one person is not doing lots of things while other people are doing very little. This not only helps people to feel valued but it also varies the worship for the people who are attending and ensures that things do not go wrong because somebody has too much to do or remember.

Finally, give people things to do that they like doing. If somebody likes reading, then maybe they would like a chance to read. If somebody hates dance, then do not ask them to take part in a dance. Remember, though, to give people a chance to choose what to take part in as this is not about performance, it is about prayer.

Step Sixteen:
Collecting the things that you need

Worship runs smoothly when you have everything you need in the right place at the right time.

Now you are almost ready to lead your worship. You have planned it carefully and you know who is going to be responsible for the different things. You will have arranged a time and place with your teacher or catechist. The only thing left to do is to collect together the things you need for your worship to run smoothly.

This just takes a little bit of thinking about. You don't want to get to a point in your worship where you need to use something, such as a candle or a piece of music, and realise that you do not have it with you.

While all worship will be slightly different, here is a checklist of some of the things that you might need.

- Everything for your focus

- PowerPoint presentation and computer set up

- The Word of God – opened at the right page so you do not have to find it during the worship

- Music – CD player, iPod or computer. If using a pianist then ask (politely) if they have the right music

- Any extra readings

- Prayers

- Anything extra you need such as candles, artwork or flowers.

It is a good idea to write a checklist for yourself as you are planning the worship to ensure that you do not forget anything. A checklist is provided here and a copy of it is on the disc that accompanies the book.

Have we got?	Check	Notes
Everything for the focus, including something to light the candle with		
PowerPoint and computer set up		
The Word of God opened at right page		
Everything for the music		
Extra readings		
Prayers		
A copy of the plan for every leader		
Anything else we need		

PART THREE

Resources that you can use to help you

CHAPTER 6

Building a Box of Resources

The last section talked about collecting the things you needed for your particular act of worship. If you are going to plan worship regularly, it is a good idea to have a box of resources where you keep the basic things that you need for collective worship. If you have the basics collected together in one box, then finding the extra things you need for a particular act of worship will not be too difficult or take too much time. Most of these things will be used for your focus but there are some others that you need.

The following is a list of suggestions as to what you might need in your box.

Things you will need in most acts of worship

- **A set of different-coloured drapes** that can be used to cover the table or the altar or just arranged on the floor. Some Christian churches have particular colours for different seasons and if your school is a faith school then you might want to use these colours. Generally you would need

  - Green for nature and everyday

  - Purple for times when you want to say sorry

  - Yellow or gold for celebration

  - White also for celebration and rejoicing

  - Blue is often the colour used for Mary but you can also use it for creation to represent water.

- **A crucifix or cross.** There are many different types of these so you can choose one to suit your group.

- **A Bible**. You can choose any Bible. There are some very good children's Bibles. You may not use this Bible during the worship as you might have a copy of your reading that you are going to use, but there should be the Word of God to display on the focus.

- **Candles** and something to stand them on.

- **Matches** or something to light the candles with. (It might be that your teacher or catechist prefers to keep these and you get them at the beginning of the worship.)

- **Special prayers** such as your school prayer.

Other things you could add

There are things you could add to give you some choice or variety when you are creating your focus or planning your worship. You may not need these things but it is useful to have them to hand when you do, so putting them in the box is a good idea.

- **A bowl or jug** to hold water in case you want to pour water or have water as part of your focus.

- **Stones, shells or pebbles** that can be used to add to the focus to represent mistakes we have made, or part of creation.

- **Statues:** your school may be named after a saint and you may have a statue or picture of that saint. You do not have to use religious statues, though; there are many lovely statues representing family or a circle of friends that you might have in your school or church.

- **Vases** or jugs to hold flowers.

Other things you might need such as flowers or plants you cannot keep in your box of resources as they would die but, if you have the basics ready, then collecting the other things is much easier.

Things you might add at different times of the year

All of the things already mentioned will help build your basic box. These are the resources you will need most often. It is useful, though, to add things at different times of the year. The Church follows a cycle throughout the year and, even if your school is not connected to a church, some of these events we all celebrate, such as Christmas and Easter.

For this reason it is handy to add a few things that you might want as a season approaches and then take them out again when the season is over. If you do this, then your box does not become too cluttered or too big and heavy. Remember the idea is that the box is to help you to organise your own worship and therefore should be something that you keep tidy and can store and carry to the places you need it.

Ideas for different times of the Church's year

Advent – *for Advent choose your purple cloth*

- **An Advent wreath:** You may not be able to keep this in your box as it may be too big, but you might want access to one.

- **A Jesse or prayer tree:** This is not a proper tree. It just needs to be something that can stand up on its own and that you can hang prayers or pictures on.

- **Words written on cards or a poster:** The words could say *Waiting* or *Preparing* as these are both themes during Advent.

Christmas – *for Christmas choose your white or golden cloth*

- **A crib:** There are many cribs to choose from. You will probably have one in school or church but you may want a small one that you can use on your focus.

- **Extra candles:** These could be used to show celebration.

- **Words written on cards or a poster:** These could say *Rejoice* or *Jesus is born*.

- **Gifts:** Remember that the Epiphany is in the Christmas season and the wise men brought gifts. You could have something to represent the gifts you bring to Jesus as part of your worship.

Lent - *for Lent choose your purple cloth*

- **Stones or pebbles:** These could represent our mistakes and the things we are trying to overcome during our Lenten journey.

- **Seeds:** These could be planted or just displayed to show that we can make new beginnings.

- **Words written on cards or a poster:** The words could say *Prepare, Stay Awake, Repent* or *Forgive*. All of these would be suitable.

Easter – *for Easter choose your white or golden cloth*

- **Flowers**: These will represent the new life that Jesus brings.

- **A picture of the risen Jesus:** This can be any picture – one you have drawn yourself or one from a book.

- **A white cloth draped around an empty crucifix:** This shows that Jesus is risen and is often a symbol used in church.

- **Words written on cards or a poster:** The words could say *Alleluia, New Life, Joy* or *Rejoice*.

May – *some churches honour Mary in May. If you want to do this, use a blue cloth*

- **A statue of Mary:** If you do not have a statue you might want a picture.

- **A set of rosary beads** if the people in your school or church use them.

- **Pictures of mothers with their children:** These can be from anywhere – you could use drawings or photographs or pictures from books.

Pentecost – *for Pentecost use a red cloth*

- **Flames drawn on card and coloured red and yellow:** You might want to write the gifts of the Holy Spirit or the gifts you have on these.

Ideas for different times of the school year

You might not always be following the Church's year when you plan your worship. You might be celebrating something else, such as spring or the beginning of term. The following are different things that might be helpful at these times of the year.

Beginning of term

- **Extra candles** so that each class can take one to their own class prayer corner.
- **New books, pencils or balls** to show how you will learn and play together during the term.

End of term

- **Completed work** from the term to celebrate the learning you have all done.
- **Collection boxes or posters** from charities that you have supported during the term.
- **Copies of certificates** to show achievements and use of your gifts.

The beginning and end of term will be very special times for your school and there will be things that you want to use that cannot be listed here, as they are special to your school. Always remember that worship is about life – and your worship is about *your* life, so do not be afraid to include things that celebrate you and your school.

Ideas for the different seasons

Spring: *for spring you could use a green cloth*

- You may want seeds, water and pictures of new life, such as baby animals or flowers to add to your focus.

Summer: *for summer you could use a yellow cloth*

- You may want pictures of summer, items to do with relaxation and recreation, such as buckets and spades or bats and balls.

Autumn: *for autumn you could use a red or orange cloth*

- You may want dried leaves and things such as acorns or conkers. Pictures of autumn colours or autumn bulbs to plant might be helpful.

Winter: *for winter you could use a white cloth with green for contrast*

- You might want fir cones or bare branches. Pictures of snow or wintry scenes could be helpful. These could be used to celebrate the beauty of winter or to show people enjoying themselves in winter.

Finally – it's your box!

The box of resources is your box, so you decide what goes into it. You might have something that you especially want or something that is special to your class or school. Be creative when you build the box. And remember – it is something that can be changed. If you realise, after you have created two or three acts of collective worship, that you do not need something that is in the box then take it out. If you need something regularly that you do not have, then put it in.

CHAPTER 7

Planning Sheets for Collective Worship

On the next few pages are different templates for you to use to help you plan your collective worship. The first ones are to plan very short acts of collective worship, as you might want to try something short to begin with. They are followed by several different planning sheets. You should use the one that you think will help you the most. You might not always choose the same one.

   Copies of the sheets are on the CD which is at the back of the book so that you can print them off and write on them.

How much should I write?

You only need to do enough writing for everyone to be sure what they are doing. Once you have decided on the planning sheet you want to use, it is a good idea for everyone who is taking part in leading the liturgy to have a copy.

Planning sheet 1:
A short act of worship
based around a Bible reading

This sheet, which is on the following page, is very simple and just allows for choosing the Word of God and sharing what it means for us today in the *Explaining the Word* section. An opening and closing prayer start and finish the worship.

The main part of the planning sheet is divided into three sections – the first column being already filled in and showing the part of the worship you are planning. The middle column is where you write what you intend to do – which Bible reading, how to explain the Word etc., and the third column is where you write who is actually going to do the different things.

This type of short worship would be suitable for class-based worship where you might already have a prayer corner or prayer focus. If not, you could light a candle and place a crucifix somewhere it can be seen.

It is suitable when you are new to planning collective worship as it has few steps and is very short.

Once you are used to planning in this way, you can develop your worship.

Planning sheet 1	Theme	
Who is attending		
Names of leaders		
Stage of worship	**What you are going to do**	**Who is doing it**
Opening Prayer		
The Word of God		
Explaining the Word		
Closing prayer		

Planning sheet 2:
A slightly more complex act of worship

This is a little more complex than the first planning sheet and allows the people attending to take part a little more.

Again it would be suitable for a class-based act of worship or perhaps a Key Stage assembly. To make it less complicated than a full act of collective worship, there is no mention of preparing a focus. If you are in class you may already have some focus that you could use that would be suitable for prayer.

There is an extra section for notes in this planning sheet. This is in case you want to add a few details or jot down anything you want to remember. If you decided that you wanted to create a small focus, then you could use this section to list what you need to collect.

Planning sheet 2	Theme	
Who is attending		
Names of leaders		
Stage of worship	**What you are going to do**	**Who is doing it**
Welcome and introduction		
Opening prayer and/or hymn		
Word of God		
Explaining the Word		
Prayer or hymn for all as response to Word		
Closing prayer		
Notes		

Planning sheets 3 & 4:
A Complete Act of Worship

There are two planning sheets suggested here. Both guide the planning of a more complex act of worship.

The first is the one you have already seen in chapter 3 which was used to give an example of planning a liturgy. This one allows you to think of different aspects of the liturgy – what you want the atmosphere to be like, etc. It does not give you the order in which you should do things. There is an example of how to use this sheet in chapter 4 which begins on page 61.

The second sheet allows you to include other details, such as who is going to take charge of the different sections. Because it will allow for a longer and more complicated act of worship, there are questions and suggestions to guide you in the section that you will fill in yourself. On the disc at the back of the book there are two versions of this planning sheet. One has the questions and looks exactly like this one. You can use this for guidance. The other is a blank copy for you to fill in yourself.

While these planning sheets allow you to write down all the building blocks you want to include and give the details, such as who is going to do the different parts, it is still up to you to decide the order in which you want to do them.

Planning sheet 3

Theme:

People attending:

What kind of collective worship:

The Word of God:

Explaining the Word:

Prayer:

Other things to include:

Focus:

Planning sheet 4	Theme
Who is attending	
Names of leaders	

Stage of worship	What you are going to do	Who is doing it
Welcome and introduction	*Hymn* *Opening Prayer* *Introduction of theme*	
Word of God	*What reading will you choose? How is it being shared? (Reading, images etc.)*	
Explaining the Word	*How will you relate it to today?* *Drama, dance, talking, etc.*	
Response to Word	*E.g. reflection, prayer, procession of items, hymn*	
Any other actions or building blocks	*E.g. giving something out, lighting candles, pouring water, planting seeds*	
Prayers and hymns/songs	*Any other prayers or music you want to include, e.g. bidding prayers*	
Ending of worship	*E.g. final prayer or hymn, any thanks you want to express*	
Items for focus	*List the things you will use to create your focus*	
Other responsibilities	*E.g. setting up focus, playing music, welcoming people as they arrive, organising PowerPoint presentation.*	

Planning sheet 5

This final planning sheet is divided into two sections. This is so that you can first plan your content and then order the service. That means to decide what order you want to do things in.

Both sections are on the same sheet which means that you only have a small space to write in. In case you feel that this is not enough space, the planning sheet is then given spread over two pages. The first page gives you space to plan what you want to do while the second gives you space to decide what order you want to do it in and who is going to lead the different sections.

Remember what it said at the beginning of this section. You only need to do enough writing for everyone to be sure what they are doing. Once you have decided on the planning sheet and filled one in, then you need to make sure that everyone who is taking part in leading the liturgy has a copy.

In chapter 11 which starts on page 153 there are examples of planning liturgy using all of these sheets.

Planning sheet 5	Theme	People attending

Names of leaders

Stage of worship & what you will do	Order of worship	Who is doing this?
Word of God		
Explaining the Word		
People's response to the Word		
Prayers		
Hymns and music		
Symbolic actions		
Items for focus		
Other jobs		

5a	Theme	People attending

Names of leaders

Stage of worship & what you will do

Word of God

Explaining the Word

People's response to the Word

Prayers

Hymns and music

Symbolic action

Items for focus

Other jobs

5b	Theme	People attending

Names of leaders

Order of worship	Who is doing this?

CHAPTER 8

Bible readings to suit different themes

When you first start planning collective worship, it is sometimes difficult to decide which Bible reading is the right one for the theme of your worship. This chapter suggests a list of themes you might want to use and it also gives suggestions as to which Bible readings might be suitable for each theme. Each reading has a reference next to it to show you where to find it in the Bible. You probably use a children's Bible in your worship most of the time so you may not need the references. The stories in a children's Bible are written especially for children to understand so they are very suitable for your own worship. You will notice that there is sometimes more than one reference. That is because you can find this reading in more than one Gospel.

Major feasts of the Church's year have their own readings but I have included these at the beginning for schools that do not follow a particular Church but want a suitable reading.

After this I have listed some more general themes that can be used at any time of the year. Some themes are similar and so some readings can be used for more than one theme. To make it easier to use, a lot of different themes have been suggested here even though some are alike. You do not have to use any of these themes though. You may want to choose your own. These are only here to help.

Season	Reading	Bible reference
Advent	Isaiah foretells the birth of Jesus: "The people who walked in darkness have seen a great light."	Isaiah 9:2-7
	The Annunciation – when the angel tells Mary she is to have a baby	Luke 1:26-38
	The Magnificat – Mary's prayer of praise	Luke 1:46-55
	The Visitation – where Mary rushes to tell her cousin, Elizabeth	Luke 1:39-45
	Jesus tells his followers to stay awake as we do not know when the Lord is coming	Mark 13:33-37
	John the Baptist	Mark 1:1-8; John 1:6-8
Christmas/ Epiphany	Joseph is told by an angel that Mary is expecting a special baby	Matthew 1:18-25
	The journey to Bethlehem	Luke 2:1-5
	Jesus is born	Luke 2:6-7
	The visit of the Shepherds	Luke 2:8-20
	The visit of the Wise men	Matthew 2:1-12
Lent	The temptations in the desert	Matthew 4:1-11; Mark 1:12-15; Luke 4:1-13
	The Transfiguration	Matthew 17:1-9; Mark 9:2-10; Luke 9:28-36
	Palm Sunday – Jesus enters Jerusalem on a donkey	Matthew 2:1-11; Mark 11:1-10; Luke 19:28-40
	Holy Thursday – Jesus washes the feet of the disciples	John 13:1-15
	Holy Thursday – The Last Supper – Jesus breaks the bread and shares the wine	Matthew 26:26-28; Mark 14:22-24; Luke 22:14-20

	Good Friday – the story of Jesus' arrest, his trial and his crucifixion is told in all of the Gospels. A story from a children's Bible would be the best thing to use as the readings in the Gospels are too long and complicated for children's worship. The chapter references are given here in case you want to find them.	Matthew 26:36 to end & chapter 27; Mark 14:32 to end & chapter 15; Luke 22:39 to end & chapter 23; John chapters 18 & 19
Easter	The tomb is empty – Jesus is risen	Matthew 28:1-10; Mark 16:1-8 & 9-11; Luke 24:1-9; John 20:1-17
	Jesus appears to his disciples	Luke 24:13-35 & 36-43; John 20:19-29 & 21:1-14
Pentecost	The Holy Spirit comes down upon the disciples	Acts 2:1-11
	Jesus gives the Holy Spirit to his disciples	John 20:19-23

The following pages show themes you could have at any time of the year. Some of them are similar and, when you are used to planning worship, you will probably see that some of the readings could be used for different themes.

Only one Bible reference is given for them all, although some of them appear in more than one Gospel. Again, wherever possible, choose a children's version of the Bible as it will be easier to understand for the people who are attending your liturgy.

Theme	Reading	Bible reference
Love	The Lost Sheep The greatest commandment Love one another as I have loved you	Luke 15:1-7 Matthew 22:35-40 John 15:12-17
Gifts	The visit of the Wise men The widow's mite The coming of the Holy Spirit	Matthew 2:1-12 Luke 21:1-4 Acts 2:1-11
Kindness/ Helping others	*There are many stories of kindness and helping you can choose. These are just a few.* The feeding of the five thousand Jesus heals the blind man The Marriage at Cana The Good Samaritan Raising of Jairus' daughter	 Mark 6:34-44 Mark 8:22-25 John 2:1-11 Luke 10:25-37 Mark 5:21-24 & 35-43
Healing	Jesus heals the lepers Jesus heals the blind man Jesus heals the paralytic	Luke 17:11-19 Mark 8:22-25 Mark 2:1-12
Friendship	Jesus raises Lazarus Jesus heals the paralytic	John 11:1-44 Mark 2:1-12
Being chosen/ Being a disciple/ Being special	Calling the disciples The calling of Samuel The calling of Abram Noah is called to build an ark	Matthew 4:18-22 1 Samuel 3:1-10 Genesis 12:1-3 Genesis 6:13-22
Forgiveness/ Being sorry/ Repentance	Zacchaeus The woman who washed the feet of Jesus Peter is sorry for denying Jesus Jesus forgives the thief on the cross The Prodigal Son	Luke 19:1-10 Luke 7:36-38 Luke 22:54-62 Luke 23:39-43 Luke 15:1-3 & 11-32
Leading or guiding others	The Beatitudes The Ten Commandments Don't hide your light	Matthew 5:1-12 Exodus 20:1-17 Matthew 5:14-16
Serving others	Jesus washes the feet of his disciples	John 13:1-15

The final set of ideas are for acts of collective worship that would be suitable for particular times of the school year.

There are a few empty rows at the end for you to add your own ideas if you want.

Season	Reading	Bible reference
Beginning or end of term	The calling of the disciples The greatest commandment	Matthew 4:18-22 Matthew 22:35-40
Spring/new life	Jesus rises from the dead The story of creation	John 20:1-17 Genesis 1:1-31
Mary/May	Mary is visited by an angel Mary visits Elizabeth Jesus is born Mary asks Jesus to help at a wedding Mary weeps at the foot of the cross	Luke 1:26-38 Luke 1:39-45 Luke 2:6-7 John 2:1-11 John 19:25-27
Harvest/ September	The story of creation Finding God in the gentle breeze Psalm 96	Genesis 1:1-31 1 Kings 19:10-13 Psalm 96
Summer/ the fullness of life	I am the Way, the Truth and the Life Psalm 19 verses 1-4 Jesus says he has come so that we have life to the full	John 14:1-6 Psalm 19:1-4 John 10:7-10
Remembrance/ November	Jesus promises to prepare a place for us Jesus rises from the dead Jesus raises Lazarus Jesus raises Jairus' daughter	John 14:1-6 John 20:1-17 John 11:1-44 Mark 5:21-24 & 35-43

CHAPTER 9

Explaining the Word – Exploring Bible Readings

You know from chapter 1 where we talked about the building blocks of collective worship, that explaining the Word is important. We must always ask ourselves what the reading means for us today. If you are planning and leading the worship then that is your job.

You will be used to people explaining the Word for you in school or perhaps at church. Teachers and catechists will spend a lot of time thinking of the best way to explain the reading to you and, because of this, you will find that working out the meaning for yourself is not too difficult. To help you get started, there are some suggestions on the following pages about how you could explain the meanings of some of the readings we have chosen. The readings in this chapter match the readings in the previous chapter, so you can use them when you first start to plan and lead worship. If a reading is used more than once, you need to look back in this section to find it.

All of the ideas can be used in different ways. You could just talk about them, explaining them in words. You could make up and act out a play or use a still image or freeze-frame pictures while you speak. There are different ideas in chapter 1 in the section on *Explaining the Word* which starts on page 30.

Remember two things. Always think about the age of the people attending the worship when you are planning what to do and ask yourself what will be most effective for them. Also, always bring the message back to the children. How are they living this message out in their daily lives today?

Reading	Ideas for Explaining the Word
Advent	
Isaiah – *Isaiah foretells the birth of Jesus. "The people who walked in darkness have seen a great light."* *This is about hearing news that fills you with joy.*	To explain it you could think of a time when you received good news and it changed the way you felt. Then, explain it to others or make up a play to show it. Finally, ask the children to do the same.
The Annunciation – *when the angel tells Mary she is to have a baby.* *The angel brings good news and tells Mary she is a special person.*	To explain this you could think of times when you have been chosen as a special person – what special job does God have for you? Then show this through drama or art. Finally ask the children to reflect for themselves.
The Magnificat *This is Mary's prayer of praise to God when she finds out that she is going to have baby Jesus.*	To explain this you could make up a litany or a prayer of praise for the things that God has given you in your life. Ask other children to reflect on this and name what God has given them. You could make up a dance to praise God.
The Visitation – *where Mary rushes to tell her cousin, Elizabeth.* *This is about sharing good news.*	To explain it you could make up a play to show sharing good news today. Try to show that when you experience the joy of sharing and the joy that good news brings, you experience the joy of God.
Stay Awake *as you do not know when the Lord is coming.* *This is telling us that we should always try to be the best person we can.*	To explain this you could make up a play or explain in words about somebody not trying their best and missing out on something.
John the Baptist *This is about somebody preparing the way for Jesus.*	To explain it you could show or talk about getting ready for somebody special coming. Ask the children to think about how important it is to prepare and what a special person John must have been to be chosen to prepare for Jesus.

Christmas **Joseph is told by an angel that Mary is expecting a special baby.**	This is about how Joseph has to trust God and trust Mary. To explain this you could show a situation today where you have to believe in somebody and link that to believing in God.
The journey to Bethlehem *This explains how Joseph and Mary have to travel to Bethlehem to be counted in the census.*	This is about a journey. To show what it means today, you could use the theme of how sometimes we have to move out of our comfort zone to achieve something and it is not easy but we must trust in God.
Jesus is born *This tells the story of the birth of Jesus.*	There are lots of ways to talk about this. You could talk or act about looking for God in unexpected places – not a palace but a stable. Where do we find God today? In other people and in acts of unexpected kindness - as in the innkeeper.
The visit of the Shepherds *The shepherds were the poorest people but the angel still chose them to share the good news of the birth of Jesus.*	To explain this you could talk about finding God in the poorest people today – realising they are special just as we are and that we have a responsibility to care for them.
The visit of the Wise men *The wise men were not Jewish and this showed that God is for everybody. They brought gifts to Jesus.*	You could pick up this theme by acting out a play about the different people who we might not expect to be people chosen by God but God shows us that they are special. Another thing you could do is to bring your gifts to Jesus through dance, drama, art or singing.
Lent *The temptations in the desert* *This story is about not giving in to things we know to be wrong.*	You can explain this by showing through drama or words how sometimes we are tempted to do something that is not good but, like Jesus, we have to find the strength to say no.

The Transfiguration *This story is about Jesus being changed.*	You can link this to moments in people's lives today when they do more than they think they are able to. It is God's love and strength that helps them. You can do this through words, drama, art or dance.
Palm Sunday - *Jesus enters Jerusalem on a donkey* *This story is about celebration.*	To explain it you can show how you celebrate today and in that celebration there is the love and praise of God. You can do this through words, drama, art or dance.
Holy Thursday – *Jesus washes the feet of the disciples* *This story is about service.*	To explain it you can show how you serve other people today and when you do you are responding to Jesus' command to copy him. You can do this through words, drama, art or dance.
Holy Thursday – *The Last Supper* *This story is where Jesus blesses the bread and wine and shares them.*	You can explain it by showing how in sharing meals today we are sharing God's love. You can link this with the Eucharist in church.
The story of Good Friday *This is a story of sacrifice where Jesus gave everything for us.*	You can talk about or show how we all must sacrifice things for others at times and, when we do, we are trying to follow Jesus.
Easter **The tomb is empty – Jesus is risen** *This is the joyful story about Jesus rising from the dead.*	To link it to today for the children you could focus on joy and use a story of joy today. Another theme you could choose is hope – by rising from the dead Jesus gave everybody a new hope. You could act or tell a story about hope in your life today. Another thing you could do is a dance or a song of praise to thank God for his gift of life.
Jesus appears to his disciples *When Jesus appeared to his disciples it was to reassure them that he was alive and then to give them a mission – to carry on spreading his message.*	You could choose either of these themes. You could use the theme of hope as for the above reading or you could explore how we might spread God's message today.

Pentecost	The disciples went out and spread the good news of Jesus. You could use this theme just like in the previous reading but another lovely theme to use at Pentecost is gift. You could act or dance or read or use art to show how you use your gifts today to spread God's love.
The Holy Spirit comes down upon the disciples	
This is a story about how the disciples received the Holy Spirit and lost their fears.	
Jesus gives the Holy Spirit to his disciples	You could use the theme of promise – how you promise something and then keep your word as Jesus did, or you could use the theme of support – how you support your friends and do what you can to help them. Choose how you will give this message to the people at your liturgy.
This tells us how Jesus promises to send the Holy Spirit to his disciples.	
Love	You could tell or act out a story about being lost and show how happy people feel when they are found. You can show how much the person who is looking for them will search until they are found. Link this to the love that God has for us.
The Lost Sheep	
This is a story about how much God loves us.	
The greatest commandment	You can use the theme of love and explain how you show your love for God by loving each other. There are lots of ways you can do this – e.g. plays about acts of kindness. Remember to make the link between this and loving God. You could try this a different way by showing how somebody said they loved God but was mean to others. You would need to explain that this person was wrong.
A lawyer asks Jesus which is the greatest commandment and he says to love God and to love each other.	
Jesus said, "Love one another as I have loved you."	This is a lovely theme to use because you can make up many stories or plays showing love or use songs or dances which are about love. Include the idea that love is about giving and sometimes needs us to give something up or do things that are difficult.
Jesus tells his disciples how important love is and asks them to follow his example.	

Gifts **The Visit of the Wise men**	Explained in the Christmas section
The widow's mite *This is a story that shows how somebody searches for something that is important even though it is small.*	You could tell a story about losing something very precious and how you searched and worried until it was found. You could then link this to how you are so precious to God that he will search for you if you wander away from him by doing the wrong thing.
The Holy Spirit comes down on the disciples	Explained in the Pentecost section
Kindness/Helping others **The feeding of the five thousand** *This tells us how Jesus performed a miracle to feed lots of people using five small loaves and two fishes that a small boy gave him.*	There are different themes to choose from in this story of Jesus. One is to focus on the fact that Jesus saw what the people needed and gave it to them. Another is to focus on the way the little boy was willing to share everything he had with others. Both of these would fit in with the themes of helping others or of kindness.
Jesus heals the blind man *This is a story of kindness where Jesus heals a man who cannot see.*	Jesus helps the man to see, so you can use the theme of helping us to see things clearly. Sometimes we don't want to do that because we have to face our faults so a story about facing up to mistakes would suit this theme. You could also use the theme of healing – helping somebody to get over something difficult.
The marriage feast at Cana *Jesus helps a couple at their wedding when the wine runs out.*	One theme you could use from this is the fact that Jesus helped people without asking for anything in return. Another is that he did what his mother asked because Mary was the one who asked him to help. You could focus on the fact that Jesus made a difference and ask when we do that.

The Good Samaritan *This is a story that Jesus tells people to show them that they should not judge others and be prejudiced against them. There is often more to people than you think.*	You could use the theme of prejudice to explain this story. The people who were listening to Jesus did not like the Samaritans and so the fact that Jesus chose a Samaritan to be the one who helped the man was very important. You could tell a story or make up a play to show that prejudice is wrong and that people who are unkind to others because they are different are making a bad choice.
The Raising of Jairus' daughter *The daughter of a man called Jairus has died and Jesus brings her back from the dead, causing great rejoicing.*	Again this story shows kindness and you could use this theme for your explanation. Jesus sees what needs doing and he does it. You could also talk about, act or dance a story about the joy that helping others will bring.
Healing **Jesus heals ten lepers** *Ten men who are suffering from a terrible and infectious disease are cured by Jesus.*	This story has many themes you could use to tell people how important it is for us today. One is the theme of kindness, another is of bravery – Jesus was brave to go near the lepers when they were so ill. You could show somebody being brave and helping others today.
Jesus heals the blind man	Explained in the kindness section. For the theme of healing you would need to use the second suggestion.
Jesus heals the paralytic *Jesus heals a man who is unable to walk. He forgives his sins and then gives him the ability to walk again.*	While you cannot heal people who are ill, you could use the theme of healing. Jesus forgives the man's sins. You could tell or act a story about the healing power of forgiveness – when you forgive somebody who has hurt you and make friends again.

Friendship **Jesus raises Lazarus** *Jesus is told that Lazarus is ill. He waits before going and Lazarus dies. Jesus brings him back from the dead.*	While you cannot raise people from the dead, you can use the theme of new life – explaining that believing in Jesus and following his ways gives us new life. Jesus said to untie Lazarus from the cloths he had been buried in. You could ask the children what it is that they need to let go of if they are to follow Jesus – perhaps selfishness, greed, anger or unkindness. You can simply talk about this or use art or still images to explain what you mean.
Jesus heals the Paralytic *A man's friends go to a lot of trouble to help him.*	Explained in the healing section For the theme of friendship you should focus on the trouble the man's friends went to in order to help him – lifting the roof so that they could lower him down. You could use this theme of going to a lot of trouble to help others. You could also look at helping people overseas through organisations such as Christian Aid or CAFOD.
Being chosen/Being a disciple Being special **Jesus chooses the disciples** *Jesus calls people to follow him.*	All of the next four readings are about being willing to recognise what you can do and being brave enough to do it. It is the call to be special and to recognise your gifts. This is about the calling to follow Jesus. Today he calls you. What can you do to follow him? Give examples, such as people helping others, people showing kindness, etc.
The calling of Samuel *Samuel hears God calling him to serve him.*	Samuel was chosen by God but at first he didn't realise it. You could use the theme of having somebody recognise something in a person that they do not see in themselves – maybe a gift of leadership or of a talent for organising and helping others. You could also use the theme of being chosen for a special job and really working hard to achieve it.

The calling of Abram *God asks Abram to leave his father's house and set off to a new land that God will show him.*	You could use the qualities of trust and courage as your theme: that sometimes we have to be brave enough to try something even though we don't know whether we will succeed. You could use examples of famous people such as Mother Teresa but also challenge the people at your worship to think what they might be called to do.
Noah is called to build an ark *God tells Noah he is going to destroy the things on the earth but that Noah must build an ark to save himself, his family and some of the animals.*	For your theme you could show that Noah trusted God to save him but knew that he had to play his part. Building an ark must have been really hard work but Noah still said yes. You could explain that if you want to achieve something – e.g. being kinder – you cannot just expect God to make you kinder – you need to work at it too.
Forgiveness **Repentance/being sorry** **The story of Zacchaeus** *Zacchaeus is chosen by Jesus and he changes his ways.*	For the next five readings you could use the theme of how giving somebody a second chance can make them a better person. This theme of giving somebody a second chance would be very suitable here. Make up an example such as a bully who is changed when he or she gets the chance to have a real friend.
The woman who washed the feet of Jesus *A woman is sorry for her mistakes and does something to show her love for Jesus and to say she is sorry.*	One theme you could use here is making amends. Think of a situation where somebody has done something wrong and tries to make up for it. Try to show the happiness that results when you have said sorry.

Peter is sorry for denying Jesus *Peter is afraid and pretends that he doesn't know Jesus and later he is sorry.*	Sometimes fear can make us do things that later we are ashamed of. You could use the theme of telling lies because you are afraid to own up to something but then finding the courage to make it right.
Jesus forgives the thief on the cross *One man who is crucified with Jesus is sorry for his mistakes.*	The theme of forgiveness is a very powerful one to use here. Despite his own pain, Jesus still was kind. A story or a play about the power of forgiveness – in our case not only for the one who has made a mistake but also for the one who is forgiving – would be effective. Show how forgiveness brings peace to both sides. You can use a familiar situation to make up a story or a play.
The Prodigal Son *Jesus tells the story of a son who leaves. Later he is sorry and comes back to make amends.*	There are several themes here. You can choose the image of the father forgiving the son and use ideas described in the previous reading. Make links between the father and God or the father and us and how important it is for us to forgive. You could choose the image of the son who is sorry and will do anything to make it up to the father for leaving and hurting him.
Leading or guiding others **The Beatitudes** *This is a set of teachings that Jesus tells his followers, showing them what kind of people they should be.*	You can choose any of the eight things that Jesus says but some are easier to explain than others. Choose *Blessed are the meek* and use the theme of trying not to be proud or to show off. Choose *Blessed are those who hunger and thirst for what is right* and use the theme of justice – try to be fair and the kind of person who makes sure that others get fair treatment.

	Choose *Blessed are the merciful* and use the theme of forgiveness. If you are not willing to forgive then you will become a hard and bitter person. Choose *Blessed are the peacemakers* and use the theme of people who always work for peace and look for a peaceful solution.
The Ten Commandments *Moses receives the Ten Commandments from God.*	One theme you could draw from this is the theme of rules. We have to have rules if we are to live in peace together. Just like the Ten Commandments, rules have to be based on what is most important. You could look at your school rules – even if you are a group in church you will be at school somewhere. Show how they were created to care for you just as God gave the Commandments to care for his people.
Don't hide your light *Jesus tells people to let their light shine.*	This is a lovely theme and can be used exactly as it is. Choose examples of how you can let your light shine today – by using your gifts, by helping others or just by being the best person you can be. You could think of something good you have done together recently – e.g. raising money for a charity – and link this to what Jesus said.
Serving others *Jesus washes the feet of his disciples.*	This is a great example of service. It is also a great example of not being too proud to do something for others because Jesus did a job that a servant would do, even though he was the Lord. You could use either of these themes. Use any example of service – a small one that you could do every day or a bigger one such as people do who go overseas to help others.

Faith **Healing the Centurion's Servant** *A man asks Jesus to help but believes in him so much that he says that Jesus only needs to speak for his servant to be healed.*	The theme of faith or belief is strong in this story. Use it to explain how God will help us to believe in ourselves or in others if we ask him. You could focus on parents or carers in this worship and show how we believe in their love for us and their willingness to help us. Bring this back then to the people at the worship. Do they believe in themselves? Who will they help?
The woman who touched the cloak of Jesus *A woman who needs healing believes that she will be healed just by touching the cloak that Jesus is wearing.*	The theme for this can be the same as the one in the previous reading. A different way to explain it would be to focus on how belief can achieve many things. You could look at a story of a famous person who trusted in God, such as one of the saints. If your school or church is named after a saint, you could choose this one. Then you could bring it back to the people at the worship by challenging them to think about what they could achieve if they believe in the power of God working in them.
Accepting others/tolerance **Jesus meets a Samaritan woman at the well.** *Jesus talks to a Samaritan woman even though Jewish people did not mix with them.*	Jesus did not ignore this woman just because she was a Samaritan as most Jews would have done. Link this with today by using the idea of not leaving people out just because they are different (colour, disability, being new, etc.). You could use a simple story about the playground or you could use a more well-known person, such as Nelson Mandela or Dorothy Day. Remember to bring it back to the people at the worship and challenge them not to be prejudiced.
Zacchaeus	Explained in the Forgiveness section. Use the idea that Jesus called to him even though other people did not like him.

Working together **We are all one body in Christ** *St Paul tells us we all have a different job to do but we are all important.*	This is an easy theme to explain. You can use the idea of everybody having different gifts and using them to make a better world. Everybody's gifts should be valued and everybody should appreciate other people's gifts as well as their own. You could explain this through words or drama or you could call out different people to help you explain how everybody is important.
I am the vine and you are the branches *Jesus tells us that if we stay connected to him we will be strong and do great things.*	You could explain that when we work with Jesus we are working for what is right. You can then extend this by showing how, when we work together for Jesus, we can achieve great things. You could use planning this worship as an example.
What is most important **I must show love** *St Paul tells us that, however gifted we are, if we do not show love then our gifts are not important.*	You could tell or act a story about two people - one who is very talented but is mean and unkind and one who is not as gifted but is very kind. Who will people most want to be friends with?
The greatest commandment	Explained in the section on Love.
Creation **The story of creation** *A story of God's love and power*	You can use this story in different ways. You can celebrate God's love and power by celebrating your favourite parts of creation and thanking God for them. You could ask children what their favourite parts are. Another way to use it is explained in the next reading.
Caring for our planet **The story of creation**	For this you could look at our responsibility for caring for the planet. You can do this in a small way by talking about picking up litter or planting seeds or in a bigger way by looking at the effect of cutting down trees and global warming.
The story of Noah	Explained in the section on Being Called. You could also focus on how Noah took different animals into the ark and link this with endangered species today.

Sharing	
The early Church shares everything *We hear how the Church shared what they had to create a community.*	You could look at the communities you belong to and explore how they share and what they share. You could then link this back to the reading by looking especially at what makes them share – common values. You could also look at sharing on a simpler level if your children are younger. What do they have to share and what will they share?
Jesus tells us to share *Jesus says, "If you have two cloaks then give one away."*	While you cannot expect children to go home and start giving away their clothes, you could ask them to think about things they have that they could share. Do they share with their brothers and sisters? Do they share with their friends? Do they have any toys they do not play with now or clothes they have grown out of that could be given away to charity? You could also use the theme explained in the previous reading.
Peace	
Isaiah says that God will guide people to turn away from war *The prophet speaks of peace.*	The theme of peace is a good one for worship as you can make up many different stories that children will recognise. Use the idea that they should be the peacemakers – find other ways to solve problems than falling out. Maybe create a play that has a difficult situation where somebody gets angry and then ask the children how they would end it.
Isaiah tells us more about peace *The prophet tells us of the peace that Jesus will bring.*	The idea of the wolf lying down with the lamb and not harming it is one of the images that Isaiah uses to show how powerful peace can be. Use this idea to show the importance of making peace with others when you have disagreed. The power of people who work for peace is great and each person needs to work for peace in their own lives. You have great opportunities for artwork here as well as other creative things.

Jesus gives us a special peace *Jesus promises us peace if we follow him.*	The theme of a special peace that comes from Jesus is a lovely one. You can use this by talking about how, when we follow Jesus, we are at peace because we know that we are doing the right thing. Also following Jesus means that we have the right priorities. We care for others, we look after our world. Things like having the right designer labels and possessions do not have high importance and this brings its own sense of peace.
Trust **"Trust in me and trust in my Father."** *Jesus tells us to trust him and that he will lead us to his Father.*	The message of this is to trust in God and that is a simple one. You can look at how we pray for people – asking God to help us. We can also look at how we follow Jesus as he tells us that he will lead us to the Father. Maybe explore this idea by widening the theme of trust and looking at when you are trusted and when you are trustworthy. You could use examples from daily life to illustrate this.
Hope **Isaiah tells us a great light will dawn** *The prophet tells of a great hope.*	Isaiah is telling us of the coming of Jesus who brought great hope into the world. The theme of how hope lights up your life can be used here. Think of something that people might hope for and show how that brings light to them. An example is when a new baby is going to be born. There is a lot of hope for the family when that happens and this brings joy.
Jesus promises to send a special friend *Jesus promised to send a special friend to his followers and that gave them hope.*	You can use the theme of making a promise here and how that promise gives hope to people. You can make up examples from daily life – e.g. somebody promising to come and visit a relative or friend, or somebody promising to take you somewhere. Another theme is to look at how friends support each other and how working together often helps you achieve more.

Jesus is transfigured *Jesus is changed as his disciples watch.*	Explained in the section on Lent. You could use the theme of Jesus being more than he seemed to his disciples. For many years they will have thought of him as a special man but here he is shown to be more. You could link this with the idea that all of us have moments in our lives when we are called to be or do more than we think we can. Link this to acts of generosity or kindness rather than achievements. You could use examples of people who create institutions like Christian Aid or Oxfam and then bring it back to the people at the worship. When might they need to do more than they think they can?
Beginning or end of term **The calling of the disciples**	Explained in the section on Being a disciple.
The greatest commandment	Explained in the section on Love.
Spring/new Life **Jesus rises from the dead**	Explained in the section on Easter.
The story of Creation	Explained in the section on Creation.
Mary/May **Mary is visited by an angel**	Explained in the section on Advent.
Mary visits Elizabeth	Explained in the section on Advent.
Jesus is born	Explained in the section on Christmas.
Mary asks Jesus to help at a wedding	Explained in the section on Kindness.

Mary weeps at the foot of the cross *Jesus asks his disciple to take care of his mother.*	This is a sad story of Mary but it has hope in it because Jesus asks his friend to look after his mother when he is dead and he asks his mother to care for his friend. You could use this theme of thinking of others even when things are not going right for you and take an example from daily life to illustrate it. You can also use the theme that Jesus will care for you even when things look really difficult.
Harvest/September **The story of creation**	Explained in the section on Creation.
Finding God in the gentle breeze *Elijah looks for God and finds him in the gentle breeze.*	You could use the theme of finding God in unexpected places for this. You could talk or tell a story about looking for God in people you do not like or do not get on with. What is good about these people? What are their gifts? If God is present in each one of us, then he is in these people too. You could also link it to the theme of harvest or creation by looking at what creation shows us of God – e.g. his beauty or power or, in this case, his gentleness.
Psalm 96 *This is a psalm of praise about how great God is and the beautiful things that God created.*	This psalm is a song of praise. When you have read it, you could make up your own song of praise about God's creation especially at this time of year. You could include people who work on the land or who work to care for God's creation – and remember that this means people too. You could dance a song of praise or you could use art to celebrate God's creation.
Summer/the fullness of life **"I am the Way, the Truth and the Life."** *Jesus tells us that he will lead us to the Father.*	You can use the theme of discipleship for this reading. You could explore how you follow Jesus and try to live by his example and his teachings. Make the link that this will lead you to the Father because you are doing what Jesus asked. You can use examples from life to illustrate your message.

Psalm 19:1-4 *The heavens declare God's glory.*	This is a simple praise of how God's glory is shown in his creation. You could use the ideas from Psalm 96 above for this reading.
Jesus says he has come so that we may have life to the full *Jesus promises that following him will bring us a full life.*	A theme to explore here is how making good choices – which is what we do when we follow Jesus – helps to fill our life with a sense of achievement and satisfaction. You can use many examples from school or daily life to show how doing the right thing brings a real sense of fulfilment and happiness to the person who is doing it.
Remembrance/November **Jesus promises to prepare a place for us** *Jesus tells us he will go ahead and we will follow him.*	This theme is good for when we remember people who have died, which we do in November. You can explore the idea that people whom we love and have died are safe with God. One way you could respond to this reading is by having a procession of names of all the people you want to remember and a short prayer to tell God that these people are important to you.
Jesus rises from the dead	Explained in the section on Easter.
Jesus raises Lazarus	Explained in the section on Friendship.
Jesus raises Jairus' daughter	Explained in the section on Kindness and Helping others.

CHAPTER 10

Music that suits different themes

Choosing the right music for your worship is important. You will know the hymns and songs you use at your school or your church, and you will also know songs and music from modern places such as films. You need to be sure that your music fits in with your theme if possible and this is not always so easy. This chapter makes suggestions about the music you could use for different themes. You may not know them all but you should be able to find them on the internet. Many of the songs are found on CDs of backing tracks. Remember though, they are only suggestions. Using what you know is always a good thing.

Season	Music suggestions
Advent	Maranatha Hail Mary Christ be our Light – Bernadette Farrell O Come, O Come Emmanuel Light the Advent Candle The angel Gabriel
Christmas/ Epiphany	Little Donkey Silent Night Away in a Manger Come, come, come to the manger While shepherds watched We three kings What shall I bring to the child in the manger? Born in the night, Mary's child Come and join the celebration The Calypso Carol It was on a starry night
Lent & Holy Week	The Servant King Shine, Jesus, shine
	Palm Sunday Hosanna to the king of kings Sing Hosanna We have a king who rides a donkey
	Holy Thursday The night before our Saviour died The Servant King The Lord Jesus
	Good Friday Were you there when they crucified my Lord? The Servant King
Easter	Christ be our Light – Easter version - Bernadette Farrell Christ the Lord is risen today Jesus, you are Lord Lord of the Dance Halle Halle Hallelujah Majesty
Pentecost	Walk in the Light Send forth your Spirit, O Lord – Liam Lawton All over the world

Theme	Music suggestions
Love	Love is his word Let there be love shared among us Love shine a light– by Katrina and the Waves Love can build a bridge – originally by The Judds A new commandment
Gift	The Gift You Are by John Denver
Kindness/ Helping others	When I needed a neighbour Share the Light – Bernadette Farrell Heal the World – by Michael Jackson
Healing	Lay your hands gently upon us Gentle as silence
Friendship	I have seen the golden sunshine Jesus is a friend of mine You've got a friend in me – from *Toy Story*
Being chosen/ Being a disciple/ Being special	You have called us by our name If I were a butterfly Here I Am, Lord
Forgiveness/ Being sorry/ Repentance	Gentle as silence God forgave my sin in Jesus' name
Leading or guiding others	Will you come and follow me? Follow Me This little light of mine
Serving others	The Servant King Here I Am, Lord Jubilate Make me a channel of your peace

Theme	Music suggestions
Faith	Faith as small as a mustard seed Jesus you are Lord Our God is a great big God
Tolerance & working together	The ink is black, the page is white Will you come and follow me? Bind us together He's got the whole world in His hands We are marching in the light of God
What is most important	A new commandment Let there be love Today is a day we've been given
Creation & caring for our planet	Morning has broken The Song of Creation The Circle of Life – from *The Lion King* Stand up, clap hands, shout thank you, Lord I have seen the golden sunshine There is a farmer
Sharing	Let there be love shared among us When I needed a neighbour
Peace	Let there be peace on earth Let there be peace shared among us Peace, perfect peace Shalom, my friends Make me a channel of your peace
Trust	Father, I place into your hands One more step along the world I go Eagles' Wings
Hope	Give us hope, Lord Our God is a great big God Lord of all hopefulness I have a dream – from *Mamma Mia*

Theme	Music suggestions
Beginning or end of term	How great is our God Follow Me A new commandment You shall go out with joy Jubilate everybody One more step along the world I go
Spring/new life	Oh Lord, all the world belongs to you One more step along the world I go
Mary/May	Born in the night, Mary's child Holy Virgin by God's decree The angel Gabriel
Summer/ the fullness of life	All things bright and beautiful Who put the colours in the rainbow? Jubilate For the beauty of the earth
Harvest/ September	Autumn Days There is a farmer The Circle of Life from *The Lion King*
Remembrance/ November	The Lord is my shepherd Oh when the saints go marching in Sometimes I wonder

CHAPTER 11

Semi-prepared worship for you to complete

This chapter has a set of planning sheets that have been partly filled in. This is to help you get started and to build up your confidence. You do not have to use them. You might feel confident enough to start from scratch and plan your own worship using the blank planning sheets in chapter 7 which begins on page 109. If you want a little help, however, these sheets will help you to plan your first acts of collective worship. General themes have been chosen as you can do these at any time of the year.

There is an example for each of the planning sheets given in chapter 7. The section where you write who the people are who are coming to your worship is not filled in because this will depend on your situation. If you are in school then adults might decide this for you to fit in with the school timetable. When you complete the planning, don't forget that you need to be sure it is suited to whoever you are leading.

Have fun finishing the planning. Use your own gifts and talents and remember to decide who is doing each section.

Planning sheet 1

This first planning sheet is very simple. You could do this in the classroom for your own classmates or as a short act of collective worship in the hall or church for a small group.

To help you, the theme of Love has been chosen. A reading has been chosen to suit the theme of love and a suggestion has been made about how you could explain the reading to others and make it relevant to their lives today.

All you need to do is to choose or write an opening prayer and decide how you are going to end your worship. You could write or choose a different prayer or you could sing a song. You could ask the children to make a promise to God to show love to somebody else during the day and then say a prayer together. You might think of a different way.

When you have done this, you need to decide who is doing the different jobs in the worship.

Planning sheet 1	Theme	Love

Who is attending	

Names of leaders	

Stage of worship	What you are going to do	Who is doing it
Opening Prayer		
The Word of God	Matthew 22:35-40 Jesus tells people what the greatest commandments are – to love God and to love one another.	
Explaining the Word	Ask the children, "How do we show that we love God?" When they have made suggestions, ask them to watch a short play. Make up a play that shows three children playing in the playground. One child gets hurt and one child laughs. The other child goes to help. Ask which child showed love for God. Explain that you show love for God by showing love for others.	
Closing prayer		

Planning sheet 2

The next planning sheet is a little more complicated. It could be used in class or as an assembly or act of worship for a Key Stage or for a small group in church. You could also lead a different class.

To start you off, the theme of being chosen has been selected. The reading where Jesus calls the disciples has been chosen to support this and a suggestion has been made as to how you could explain this to people today in the *Explaining the Word* section. The idea for this is to use still images or art to support what you are saying. If you use still images then the living pictures could change to show each of the people you have chosen doing something good or kind to follow Jesus – e.g. a picture of Mother Teresa helping the poor people in Calcutta.

All you need to do is to decide how you are going to welcome people and introduce the worship, then choose an opening prayer or hymn. If you use the suggestion about the 'Our Father' being used as a response to the Word then you need to write or choose a different prayer, or choose a hymn for the end.

Remember to decide who is taking responsibility for the different parts.

In the notes section you could add details about the four people you choose for the *Explaining the Word* section or you could decide to have a small focus and write here what you will put in it.

Planning sheet 2	Theme	Being chosen

Who is attending	

Names of leaders	

Stage of worship	**What you are going to do**	**Who is doing it**
Welcome and introduction		
Opening prayer and/or hymn		
Word of God	Matthew 4:18-22 Jesus calls the disciples	
Explaining the Word	Explain using still images or pictures about four different people who are using their gifts to follow Jesus – choose two well-known people like Mother Teresa or Nelson Mandela but also choose two from your group and show how they follow Jesus by the way they live – e.g. being kind, helping, etc.	
Prayer or hymn for all as response to Word	'Our Father' – as this explains what Jesus wants his followers to do.	
Closing prayer		

Notes

Planning sheet 3

This is a more complex act of worship and needs you to do a little more preparation than the previous two.

This one has been used as an example earlier in the book. Some of the sections have been left blank this time for you to add your own ideas. If you want to use the other ideas that were given in chapter 4, then the full plan is on page 78.

Whichever you choose, you will have to decide on the order of service – that means what order you will do things in as this plan does not organise the worship for you. It just allows you to write down all your ideas.

Planning sheet 3

Theme: Kindness to others

People attending:

What kind of collective worship: A lot of opportunity for children to join in with singing and prayer but some quiet reflection time too.

The Word of God: Jesus curing the blind man *(Luke 18:35-43)*

Explaining the Word: two short dramas showing people helping today – one at home and one by helping a charity for people overseas.

Prayer:

Other things to include:

Focus:

Planning sheet 4

This sheet is also more complex and allows you to do more varied things in your worship.

The theme that has been chosen is Friendship. The Word of God has been chosen and suggestions given for explaining the Word. To help you a little more, a suggestion has been given for how the children could respond to the Word and some symbolic action that could take place.

The rest of it is up to you. Remember to sort out responsibilities and this time that includes collecting and setting up the focus.

Planning sheet 4	Theme Friendship	
Who is attending		
Names of leaders		
Stage of worship	**What you are going to do**	**Who is doing it**
Welcome and introduction		
Word of God	Mark 2:1-12: The healing of the paralytic. We hear how the man's friends are so determined to help him that they take off the roof to bring him to Jesus.	
Explaining the Word	Have six friends come out. Three of the friends explain why they have chosen the others as their friends. You could add a short play about being a good friend.	
Response to Word	Listen or dance to 'You've Got A Friend in Me' from *Toy Story*	
Any other actions or building blocks	You could write four prayers about friends at home, overseas, friends we have lost and Jesus as a friend. Have a child light one candle to represent each group of friends as the prayers are read.	
Prayers and hymns/songs		
Ending of worship		
Items for focus		
Other responsibilities		

Planning sheet 5

This final planning sheet is given in three sections. This is explained in chapter 7 on page 119. The first sheet has two columns – one for planning and one for deciding on the order of service. This does not give a lot of room to write though, so the next two sheets have the two columns split up. When you are skilled at planning and leading your own collective worship then you might find that the first sheet is enough. The important thing when choosing how to plan is to choose the sheet that suits you best.

The theme chosen here is Faith. Again, only part of the liturgy is planned. This time I have left you to decide how to explain the Word. For the order of service the first part is done and the rest is left for you.

Planning sheet 5	Theme Faith	People attending

Names of leaders

Stage of worship & what you will do	Order of worship	Who is doing this?
Word of God Matthew 8:5-10 Healing the Centurion's Servant	Introduction and welcome	
Explaining the Word	Opening prayer	
People's response to the Word Say the Apostles' Creed or write a prayer that states what people believe in and have the children repeat it – e.g. 'We believe in justice'.	The Word of God Explaining the Word	
Prayers		
Hymns and music		
Symbolic actions Have a procession of words and pictures that show what you believe in.		
Items for focus: a Crucifix, candles, a drape, items to represent faith – e.g. a baptismal candle.		
Other jobs		

5a	Theme Faith	People attending

Names of leaders

Stage of worship & what you will do

Word of God

Matthew 8:5-10 - Healing the Centurion's Servant. We hear how the Centurion has such great faith that he tells Jesus that he does not need to come to his servant but if he only speaks a word then his servant will be healed.

Explaining the Word

People's response to the Word

Say the Apostles' Creed or write a prayer that states what you believe in and have the children repeat it – e.g. We believe in justice – **Response: We believe in justice**.

Prayers

Hymns and music

Symbolic action

Using the statements you made in the response section, collect pictures or create word art that shows these and then have children carry them in procession and place them on the focus where everybody can see them.

Items for focus:

Crucifix, candles, a drape, items to represent faith – e.g. a baptismal candle. Do not put too much on the focus if you are going to add the words and pictures later.

Other jobs

5b	Theme Faith	People attending

Names of leaders	

Order of worship	Who is doing this
Welcome and introduction	
Opening prayer	
The Word of God	
Explaining the Word	

And now you know everything you need to know, so have fun planning and leading your worship.

And now ...

back to the adults

PART FOUR

CHAPTER 12

Giving a whole class introduction

Although the idea of this book is that children can use it themselves as a guide book, I know, from years of experience as a busy teacher, that the potential to introduce the basic concept to a whole class would be extremely useful. You could then hand the book over to a group who would be already primed with an understanding of what to do and the idea of which building blocks to use.

This chapter is going to provide a script for doing that. The following notes support a PowerPoint presentation which is on the disc that accompanies the book. For that reason, these notes are organised according to the slide they refer to.

The notes are not a script to follow word for word. They are notes – stating the information that needs to be given to support each slide, thus ensuring that children get the information they need to enable them to begin planning their own worship. There is a great opportunity for discussion with the children while delivering the presentation. Nobody knows their class like the class teacher and so some people might find that they do not need to spend long on some of the slides as their children already have some knowledge. Others, however, might feel that each slide is needed.

While these notes are fairly comprehensive, the bulk of the information is in the relevant chapters in the book, and it would help children if they read the relevant sections once they set off on their own. If you do not feel too secure in teaching about leading collective worship, then the relevant chapters will give you more information to support each slide.

If you are using this just to introduce the concept of planning their own collective worship, then you only need the first three slides. The rest will explain the building blocks and the structure of collective worship.

Accompanying notes for the PowerPoint presentation
Slide 1: How to plan and lead your own collective worship

This is the cover page for the slideshow.

Slide 2: What is Collective Worship?

The first slide needs to define what we mean by collective worship and ensure that the children do not think that all assemblies, regardless of their purpose and format, are collective worship. Equally, they need to know that anything where people gather and pray together **is** collective worship, even if there are notices or other things tagged on at the end.

It then needs to explain that collective worship can have any theme. Prayerful celebrations of Harvest Festival or autumn, for instance, are just as much collective worship as worship showing repentance or marking Easter or Christmas.

Slide 3: Why plan and lead worship yourselves?

This slide needs to help children understand the enormous satisfaction you get when you plan and lead something like this and watch other people taking part and enjoying it. The sense of achievement is great. It needs to help them understand that using their own gifts to plan worship is a kind of worship in itself – using the gifts that God gave them to praise him. They also have an innate ability to make things relevant for their peers.

Slide 4: So how do you do it?

This slide introduces the children to the two basic things they need to know. The first is the components of worship. I have referred to these throughout the book as *building blocks*. The other thing they need to have some idea of is the structure of an act of collective worship – a basic understanding of the gathering, etc. You do not have to discuss either of these with the children at this point as they will be explored further in the following slides.

Slide 5: First choose your theme

This slide explains that the children's theme for collective worship can be many things. If you are following the Church's year then they might want to choose a theme that fits in with that, but for many children an abstract theme, as explained in chapter 2, can be very relevant and therefore easy to plan. Once the theme is chosen, then the rest of the components are easier to decide.

Slide 6: Then choose your building blocks

This slide explains that there are two types of building block – those that you should include in every act of collective worship and those that you can choose from.

Slide 7: Building blocks you should always include - the Word of God

This slide and the following two explore the building blocks that you should always use when planning an act of collective worship. They begin with the Word of God which should be at the heart of the worship. They need to understand that this is not about position – in the middle – but about relating everything to it. It must be relevant to the theme they have chosen and should lie at the heart of all other choices.

Slide 8: Building blocks you should always include - explaining the Word

This slide explains the need for relating the Word of God to today and to their own lives. In faith schools they will be very used to this as it will form part of their religious education lessons. If they are not used to it, then it is a skill that can be easily developed as long as you use a version of the Bible that is easy for them to understand and uses language that is familiar to them. They can do this in many ways and it gives them an opportunity to be creative – using drama or dance.

Slide 9: Building blocks you should always include – prayer and reflection

This slide explains the need to always include prayer – in whatever format they choose – and reflection. Prayer can take many different formats – e.g. words, song or dance. Reflection should always be part of worship as it gives people a chance to think for themselves and to consider their own actions and lives in the light of what they have heard. It is very important to tell the children that they must match the length of reflection to the age of the people attending the worship.

Slide 10: Building blocks you should always include – a focus

This is the last slide in this section and explains the need for a focus. When children are very new to preparing worship, then just a candle, a crucifix and a Bible are sufficient for the focus but they should get used to setting the scene. If you belong to a faith school then each classroom will probably have a prayer corner. You may have something religious in the hall which could serve as a focus and if you are in church then there will be a natural focus. If you do not have any of these, then it is good for the children to set up a simple focus where everyone can see it.

Slide 11: Building blocks you can choose from – sign and symbolic action

This slide and the following two explain the building blocks that you do not have to include but can choose from to enhance worship. The children need to know that more is not always better. Too many elements, especially in the hands of novices, could overwhelm the worship and it would lose its prayerfulness. A little guidance at first is a good thing for enthusiastic planners. Suggest that they choose one or two extra elements to begin with. The first component is sign and symbolic action. Children may have come across these in their religious education lessons. Using a sign means using something that can represent something else – such as a candle to represent Jesus as the light of the world.

Symbolic action means to do something that has a deeper meaning – such as pouring water to represent the cleansing power of forgiveness.

Slide 12: Building blocks you can choose from – music and drama

Music enhances worship, especially for children, as it gives everybody an opportunity to join in if singing, or to reflect if they are listening. In their own worship children can use a variety of music. You will probably have a series of hymns and songs that your school or group know and they can choose from these. They can also use recorded music if they want people simply to listen, or they can dance to it or use it to enhance processions or images. Not all music has to be religious but you should be sure that all lyrics are appropriate if they choose something from a film or from modern music.

Drama is a great favourite with many children and offers a visual and immediate way to understand what is being said to the people attending the worship. Drama is effective when relating the reading or the theme of the worship to today. It does not have to be a full-blown play but could simply be a series of still images that accompany somebody reading or a piece of music.

Slide 13: Building blocks you can choose from – liturgical dance and artwork

The word 'liturgical' should not put children off using dance. It just refers to dance used in worship. They will be used to dance from PE lessons as well as social activities and some children will spend time making them up in the playground or for talent shows. They should feel confident in using the same skills when making up a dance to use in worship. If they are not so confident, then a simple way to begin is to use an action song that they lead from the front. Finding a suitable song can be a little difficult and they may need your help. Suggestions as to music are given in chapter 10.

Artwork provides a visual aid for children and can be used to support any part of the worship – e.g. the Word of God, explaining the Word, etc. It can be work they have prepared themselves or it can be work by a well-known artist. It can be used to include movement by processing forward with it and then displaying it on the focus. This slide completes the explanation of the building blocks.

Slide 14: The framework for collective worship

This slide and the following five explain how to structure your collective worship. Children need some freedom when structuring their worship to allow for creativity, but a basic framework will be helpful to give some order to their worship.

Slide 15: The framework for collective worship - the gathering

This slide explains that this needs to come at the beginning. That may seem obvious to the children but they need to think about **how** they want people to gather as this will help create the atmosphere for their worship. Even if the children are just moving from their chairs in the classroom to the carpet they need to decide how they want this to happen. Quiet music playing is often a good way for them to set the scene. They may want to sing a hymn as people gather.

Slide 16: The framework for collective worship - the welcome and introduction

This slide explains that the children attending the worship need to be welcomed and the theme needs to be introduced straight after the gathering. How they explain this is up to them. They can just have one person say it or they can share it out between a few. It might be that, as they become more confident, they become more creative – e.g. they could choose a song to listen to that is relevant to their theme. They could then follow this up with a short explanation or question and answer session that draws the information out of the children attending. An example of this is to listen to the 'Circle of Life' from Disney's *Lion King* at the beginning of worship with the theme of creation.

Slide 17: The framework for collective worship – listening to or sharing God's Word.

From now these elements are in the right order but do not have to follow each other. The children can slot other things – prayers, actions etc. – in between them. This slide explains listening to or sharing God's Word. Usually this will take the form of reading but it can be done more creatively if the children feel confident – e.g. with still images to accompany it or done in parts.

Slide 18: The framework for collective worship – responding

This slide explains that children need some opportunity or vehicle through which they can respond to the reading. They can do this by simply offering a period of reflection. Another way is to write or say prayers that allow them to respond or perhaps to sing a hymn. An example of this is to say the 'Our Father' together if they have heard a reading on the teachings of Jesus about sharing. A different way is to give them something to reflect on, such as a dance for them to watch which conveys the message of the reading.

Slide 19: The framework for collective worship – the sending out

This slide explains the final part of the worship. Good worship should make a difference to us and send us out thinking about the difference it is going to make to our lives. The children can do this in different ways. An obvious one is singing a relevant hymn, but as they become more confident they may have other ideas such as giving different classes or people a lighted candle to remind them of what has gone on. In smaller acts of worship they could give out a card with a thought for the day.

Side 20: So now you are ready

This slide explains that they are now ready to plan their worship and reminds them to use their own gifts when doing so. Planning their own worship should always be something they really enjoy and using their own particular gifts – whether it be singing or drama or dance or other things – can ensure that not only do they enjoy it but that it is of good quality and other people will enjoy it too.

You could remind them finally that they should feel confident to ask for help if they are unsure about anything. They should not feel it to be a failure if they cannot do it all by themselves at first. As their experience develops, they will ask for less and less and soon will be able to be the ones who are supporting the younger children as they move up through the school or get more experience in church.

CHAPTER 13

What might you expect from different age groups?

While this book is for children to use themselves, there is clearly a lot of reading that would make it unsuitable for younger children. As stated in the introduction, it is principally aimed at Upper Key Stage Two and Lower Key Stage Three. That does not mean, though, that children should not be taking some part in contributing to the planning or leading of worship at a younger age. Basic skills can be developed and groundwork can be done lower down the school or with younger children in church, as long as children are regularly taking part in some form of worship. If they do not have experience of worship, it will be more difficult because they may not have any concept of what is religious so will not be able to make appropriate suggestions. For children who have experience of worship, their contribution can develop as they get older and more experienced.

As with anything else, the skill of planning and leading worship is cumulative; the more children do it, the better they will become. If children are used to playing even a small part in their worship from a young age, this will encourage them to feel ownership of their worship and will empower them to take responsibility for planning and leading it as they get older.

They will get a huge sense of satisfaction from it and will develop into religiously literate people who are comfortable with the language and ritual of worship.

You will know your own children best and so the suggestions offered here are simply guidelines. You may find that your children, through background or experience, are behind or ahead of the suggestions for their age group and so you should adapt them accordingly. The suggestions are organised according to school groupings but, in case you are working in church, the approximate ages have also been given.

There is no expectation that children will do everything that is suggested for their year group at once. They should at first just take one role in worship one day – for example, in Year 3 they might prepare the focus– and another on a different day – for example, another day in Year 3 they might write a prayer. The suggestions are cumulative – in that each year builds on the previous year.

For the younger children described in the first two groups – those in Foundation Stage and in Key Stage One – the worship will still be prepared and planned by the teacher or by older people but the children can make suggestions as to what can be included. They can also take part in the worship, playing roles and performing actions that will develop their confidence.

Building up leadership skills – a breakdown by year group
Very young children – Foundation Stage – aged 4 to 5

For this age group, worship will be very short so their contribution will be small but even at this young age you could ask them about things they might want to put on the focus or somebody at home that they might want to say a prayer for. This is the beginning of ownership of liturgy.

Key Stage One – aged 6 to 7

By the time children get to Key Stage One their experience of worship will have developed and they will be able to add a little more to your collective worship. At the beginning of Year 1 things they have done in Foundation stage could be reinforced – choosing things for the focus, choosing who to pray for. They could now extend this choice to include people in school.

As they come towards the end of Year 1 some of the children could begin to read very short prayers in class worship.

As they move into Year 2 they can begin to do a little more. By now they will have begun to develop a familiarity with some of the main stories of Jesus and could make a suggestion about which reading to use at the main feasts of the Church's year. They will be able to take part in short question and answer sessions about the meaning of the readings, thus sowing the seeds for *Explaining the Word*. They will be able to write short prayers and read them out during worship. They could develop their suggestions as to what you might include on the focus by explaining why certain religious artefacts should be included.

Older children – Lower Key Stage Two – ages 8 and 9

In Year 3 a good part of the worship will probably still be planned and organised by adults but the children's contribution can develop further. They will now have more experience of taking part in worship and so will be familiar with its different parts. Writing prayers and choosing people to pray for will still be part of their contribution, but now they could move to preparing the focus themselves, based on suggestions given by the adult in charge. They may already have experience of suggesting which Gospel story to use for major church feasts but could now extend that to suggestions for different themes and they could suggest hymns or songs to use. They could be asked to plan one section of the worship, such as the gathering and welcome or the sending out.

By the time they get to Year 4, their experience will be developing even more and now they can begin to plan longer sections of worship. They should be able to tackle *Explaining the Word*. They may still need a prior discussion about what the reading might mean for them today but they would easily be able to prepare short plays or artwork that showed this meaning and which they could then show to others as part of the worship. They can also choose and write prayers.

If they have taken part in worship as suggested here from the age of four, then, towards the end of the year, they will be ready to plan and lead a short act of worship for their own classmates. They will have experience of creating a focus, choosing a reading and explaining it with help, choosing or writing prayers and possibly hymns. A short act of worship can easily be planned using these skills.

Older children - Upper Key Stage Two – aged 10 and 11

The book is aimed at these children and so can be used in its entirety with these children. At the beginning of Year 5, if they already have the experience of previous years, then perhaps a short act of worship for their classmates to begin with would be a reasonable expectation. This could then be followed by an act of worship for a Key Stage.

By the time they get to Year 6 they should be planning and leading their own worship with confidence and some should be able to lead younger children.

Key Stage Three – Year 7

These students should be confident in planning and leading worship and can simply work from the book. In the current educational climate of linking schools – e.g. through academy chains, these young people could form a group that visit their primary schools to help younger children plan and lead their own worship. This would be an excellent opportunity for cooperation and developing leadership and people skills in the older students.

In church groups the older children could take a lead and encourage the younger children to be active.

A final word

It might seem a lot for them to take on – all the different building blocks and organisation – but my experience tells me that they will not only soon pick it up but will love the responsibility and the opportunity to use their skills and talents to create something. And remember – you're always around to help!